HITTING THE WALL

...and breaking through!

This book is dedicated to:

the magical books I've read

the inspiring courses I've attended

the wonderful teachers I've met and learnt so much from

the incredible students who attend our programs

the diverse and talented group of friends and family that I have

and all the amazing experiences that go towards making up this
delightful adventure called life!

Thank you!

HITTING THE WALL
...and breaking through!

Cover illustration, Book Design and Setting by Neil Coe
(neil@cartadesign.co.uk)

Set in ITC Avant Garde Gothic 9pt on 14pt

First published in 2007 by;

Ecademy Press
6 Woodland Rise, Penryn,
Cornwall UK TR10 8QD
info@ecademy-press.com
www.ecademy-press.com

Printed and Bound by;
Lightning Source in the UK and USA

Printed on acid-free paper from managed forests. This book is printed
on demand, so no copies will be remaindered or pulped.

ISBN-978-1-905823-24-6

Be the difference
that makes a difference!

Contents

1. Facing the Wall 7

   - The power of decisions

   - 1 question that could change the direction of your life

2. The Journey Begins 29

   - Preparing for the journey of creating a life

   - How to create space for new opportunities

3. Digging Deeper – tunneling through 39

   - The power of action

   - The 6 questions you forgot to ask yourself

4. Breakthrough 59

   - Instant 'feel good' boosters

   - Discover how to overcome the 'dream stoppers'

5. Climbing Over...79

   - The power to choose your own reality

   - Taking a look in the magic mirror

6. Planting seeds in the garden of opportunity 99

   - Finding the hot buttons to give you that 'kick start!'

7. Through the Wall 117

ABOUT THE AUTHOR..120

EXPERIENTIAL PROGRAMS 122

REFERENCES 123

CHAPTER 1

THE WALL

THE WALL

'Change is a door that can only be opened from the inside.'

He was the ruler of a huge empire and the time had come to seek an able and wise successor who would have all the skills and abilities to take over after he had retired. He assembled the best people he knew and asked qualified consultants to seek others in distant lands that might have what it takes.

On a particular day, all the possible successors were gathered together in a magnificent hall. The ruler addressed the gathering. 'I have a problem and I want to know who among you has the ability to solve it? What you see in the brick wall behind me is the biggest, mightiest, and heaviest door in the empire. Who among you, without help, has the power to open it?'

Some of the possible successors simply shook their heads and left almost immediately. It was just too big a problem. Others examined the door more closely, discussed different options while remembering theories of problem solving they had learned, thought about it some more before admitting defeat. It seemed an impossible task.

Have you ever felt that a task was too difficult to overcome? Have you ever felt like you've hit a brick wall, a roadblock or barrier? Or a problem was just too difficult to solve or that you're just going around in circles? Sometimes it's just a build up of a series of disappointments and setbacks that knock you off balance and it's easier to sit and wallow in the mire rather than try and stand!

Have you ever said to yourself, 'I wish I was in a relationship or in a better one,' 'I wish I knew what I wanted,' 'I wish the phone would ring,' 'I wish I had more money,' or 'if only I had a more understanding boss.' 'What should I do next?' or 'why is this happening to me?' Maybe you feel frustrated and can't figure out why. Or perhaps you want something to happen but you don't know what exactly. How can you make sure you feel happy and fulfilled? It's like being stuck in a traffic jam and you don't know what's causing the jam! Or entering a maze and wondering in which direction to turn and if you'll ever find a way out!

Since we live in a world of infinite choices and infinite opportunities, the first step – and it's an important one – is to find out what we really do want instead. After all, what is the difference between people who are successful, feel happy and fulfilled and those that don't? What is it that they are doing and that you're not doing, yet? Are you curious to find out what's going on in their heads?

I'm curious to know what questions are going around in your head right now. And I'm curious because it's been said that we can never ask a question without knowing the answer to that question. It's our own beliefs and patterns in thinking and behaviour that often prove a block in finding a way through the brick wall to the answer. And we're going to break through that wall so YOU can find your way forward.

'How did things get this way?' you may be saying to yourself. Many of us get caught up in our routines: work routine, relationship rut, fitness habits and health regime or lack of! We get caught up in the way we always do things. In other words, we sit safely in our own comfort zone. Do you find that you do the same things on a regular basis, such as making a cup of coffee as soon as you wake up in the morning, reading the paper as soon as you get to the kitchen table in the morning, buying the same brand of toothpaste, or driving the same route to the office? And have you ever experienced your car taking the route to the office when it's the weekend and you were heading for the shopping mall? Do you habitually do the same things every weekend? Do you follow the same schedule week in and week out? Do you eat the same food? Do you have the same fitness routine and wonder why you're no longer toning up or losing weight? It's as if you're on auto-pilot! This is the comfort zone and, believe me, there are a lot of good reasons to stay in the comfort zone – the routines and habits you have and the things you do every day. After all, it's safe, simple, predictable, comfortable and routine. It's stress free and there's no thinking required. Furthermore, it feels good and there are no worries or surprises!'

In Sri Lanka, you might be confused when you see huge elephants being held to a tree by a small piece of rope tied to their front leg. There are no chains or cages and it's obvious that the elephants could, at anytime, break away from their bonds but for some reason, they do not. So why is it that these huge, beautiful, magnificent creatures just stand by the tree and make no attempt to get away?

When the elephants are very young and much smaller, they use the same size rope to tie them to a tree and at that age, it's enough to hold them. As they grow up, they are conditioned to believe they cannot break away. They believe the rope can still hold them so they never even try to break free. These animals could at any time break free from their bonds but they believe they cannot and remain stuck right where they are. How many of us go through life hanging on to a belief that we cannot do something, simply because we failed at it once before?

I remember auditioning for the school choir! I loved singing and could often be found in front of a mirror with a hairbrush acting as a microphone. I practiced for hours for the audition and any nerves were wiped away by my excitement and the prospect of singing and creating harmony with the rest of the choir. What if I was picked out as a soloist? What if this led to my true calling to be the 'next big thing' in the music industry? Those questions were answered very quickly when I was rejected without reason. I'd sung barely a few lines when I was stopped and dismissed. To this day, I shy away from karaoke night due to a belief that my singing could clear the bar very rapidly!

How many of us go through life staying close to what is safe and familiar? Like the baby elephants, we too get used to staying close to what is safe and familiar. We get stuck in the shallow end of the pool and never swim further to explore the wonders of a coral reef. Just for a moment, stop and think about what's bad about those things that you do every single day? That's right! It becomes boring, monotonous and tedious. You become complacent with the way things are, losing your edge and becoming lazy.

Many people prefer to stay in the safety and predictability of the comfort zone. Their life is not brilliant, but it's not bad! If I were to ask you, right now, 'How are things going in your life?' how would you respond? And how are things going in your relationships and what about business?' What would you say? When I ask these questions in our seminars, people usually say 'OK, fine, it could be better', 'I mustn't complain' or 'fair to middling' whatever that means! Could it be better? Could YOU be better? Of course it could, and of course you could. So what's stopping you? You can dream about having more money, being in a better relationship, changing careers, buying a new car, but just thinking and dreaming about it doesn't get it, does it?!

Just for a moment, imagine a big TV screen or a small portable TV screen? Which grabs your attention the most? That's right! The big one!

Just for a moment

Most people only do something when they hit a brick wall, when they hit rock bottom, and when the problems and challenges seem to be projected onto the BIG screen. This often results in a massive wake up call and most people's goal setting or New Year resolutions are around getting away from feeling bad and stuck in their rut. They start off well. They're motivated to get away from the bad feelings so they take massive action and before too long they start to see some changes. As the situation improves, they gradually move back into their comfort zone. As if by magic, the motivation disappears, the action disappears to next to nothing and they return to the safety of the comfort zone. The majority of people live their entire lives in the comfort zone. Their life is not awful and it's not brilliant but it's not bad. That's a shame – what a waste!

If your life can be brilliant, why don't more people take action and do something about it? Every year thousands of people across the globe attend courses and buy books on goal setting, goal getting and personal development and achievement. Yet they never reach their true potential or put into practise the tools and techniques that they have learnt because they simply go back to the way they've always done things. They go back to the comfort zone and wonder why their life is not quite the way they imagined when they were younger. No doubt most of them will settle for second best and get caught in the comfort zone and in complacency.

Do this Now!

Just for a moment fast forward your life in one year's time, five years' time, ten years' time, 20 or 30 years' time when it's not turned out quite the way you imagined. Will you be regretting the things you've done or regretting the things that you didn't do? Because if you keep doing what you've always done, you'll always get what you've always got!

The human potential is to grow! Babies don't come with a manual. You only have to look at young children as they learn to walk, talk, read and write by watching others. And they ask a lot of questions! Questions to help them learn and grow, and take massive leaps forward!

As we get older, we are still learning and growing but we tend to get stuck in our habits and patterns of behaviour which can make it harder to step out of the comfort zone. ....unless we really have to!

What about buying a new mobile phone? How many of you stick with the same brand so you can skip reading the instruction manual and save the embarrassment of cutting off important calls just because you can't figure out how your new phone works? Do any of you remember sitting behind a computer screen for the first time? While I was an excellent touch typist I only learnt to use a computer because I had to. Before that, I just used to ask my friend to open up a blank page for me, then I'd type in everything I'd need to and he would have to save and close the document for me! It was only when he left that I succumbed to pressure to learn desktop publishing...and it was easier than I thought!

Ultimately, we will never be truly happy unless we are growing. Growth equals life. Look around you: on this planet, everything that is alive is either growing or dying. The growth zone is where we can go to learn, innovate, experiment and try unfamiliar things and the farther we venture into the growth zone, the greater the potential and possibilities there are for learning.

So what's it like when you first move into the growth zone?

I've lived in the Middle East for over sixteen years now and yet I still vividly remember my first day in Dubai. It was the middle of July and the first thing that hit me as I stepped off the plane and onto the sizzling tarmac was the incredible heat and humidity. Before then, I thought 'hot' was the Spanish Costa Brava in July! I was excited to be in a completely different part of the world with different sights, sounds and smells, yet anxious and curious at the same time. I also remember being surprised to find the sea temperature akin to a warm bath – really! I knew no one, and was about to start a completely new role and a new life in Sharjah. In fact, I had never even heard of Sharjah before being offered the position of Entertainment Manager at a resort hotel. Would I make new friends? Would I be homesick? Would I be able to handle my new role and responsibilities? Would I be able to settle in to a new environment? Would other people like me? And would I be able to get a decent cup of tea?!

Do you recall when you were first learning to write? It was difficult to hold a pencil let alone draw a straight line on a piece of paper. Over time, and with practice, that experience became a habit and now you can write easily and effortlessly without thinking!

If you want to get back in touch with this experience again, if you're right handed, just try writing your name with your left hand. And if you're left handed, try writing with your right hand! It will probably look like a strange alien scrawl and it will feel very strange!

Give this a go!

Do you remember your first driving lesson? I'd just turned seventeen, the legal age for driving in the UK, and even though my instructor was nicknamed 'Miserable Mitchell,' nothing could dampen my spirits. I was so excited that I could hardly wait to get into the car. There I was, safety belt buckled and in the driver's seat. First, the instructor told me to put both hands on the steering wheel. Next he told me to look down so I could see three foot pedals on the car floor under the steering wheel. 'Hmmm,' I thought, 'three pedals and I only have 2 feet,' and then he proceeded to show me the hand brake, the indicator, the gear stick, the wing mirror and side mirrors, the brake, and turn the key in the ignition... 'And don't forget to ease your foot off the brake and press gently on the accelerator,' he growled as I crunched the gears – the first of many times! Suddenly, I was into information overload...and waaay out of my comfort zone. There were times I thought I would never learn to drive a car. I was confused with all this new information. The famous hypnotherapist, Milton Erickson, once said that confusion always precedes enlightenment. And think about it, whenever you have experienced a major breakthrough in your life, did you experience confusion beforehand? Everyone has. So confusion's a good thing because it means that you are learning and changing. With time, practice...and patience, I went on to pass my driving test first time around!

In order to grow, we need to spend time beyond the borders of our comfort zone. It can feel uneasy, risky, sometimes scary, exciting and different. We have to get used to the sense of newness, the feeling of adventurousness and the initial discomfort. That's because there's not much growth in the comfort zone and not much comfort in the growth zone!

It's all about choice!

Tunnelling & Digging Deeper

Wendy was very happy, and very good in her area training role with a well-known international hotel group. She was very much in her comfort zone! She knew all the staff by name, had organised her office just the way she liked it and was used to the hustle and bustle of working within a hotel. Wendy spoke to me and said, 'To be honest, I also like the security of a regular job, monthly salary (although not good), my apartment, the travelling and the people.' We had invited her to a brainstorming brunch to discuss joining our team. It had been talked about for a long time, but she was always too busy at the hotel with new projects and new initiatives. The questions going around her head were 'Should I leave a safe job?' 'What do I really want to do next?'

She continued, 'When my new boss called me in for a chat I had no idea that he was about to rock my world and tip it over! He told me there and then that my Area role no longer existed. My jaw dropped and for a rare moment, I couldn't think of a thing to say. I had hit a brick wall and felt numb and shocked that he wanted me to take a lesser position and become merely the Hotel Training Manager. How could this be happening to me?'

'I was upset. Angry. Hurt. Tearful. Disappointed. Horrified and stunned!'

'Everything I knew, respected and loved about working for the organization had suddenly changed overnight! I talked to a few key people and shared my disappointment and anger. Did he not realise what a key role mine was? Had he not thought this through properly? Who will communicate with the area and the other general managers? Who will develop new training managers and attend the regional meetings? How could I not be needed? All these questions were going around in my head, but as the shock wore off, I realised that I really was about to lose my job. My role within the group was now redundant and I would have to move on and out of my comfort zone. Let them miss me, I thought indignantly!'

'I resisted the change at first. The way I did this was to agree to stay for a couple of months to finish projects I had started and prepare handovers of my champion roles. I tried to keep some order and routine, but each day it got harder to go to work until the point where I didn't want to be there anymore! I was ready to leave my comfort zone. It was a relief to leave!'

It's natural for people to resist change. The main reason we resist change is because all change involves something coming to an end. And with all endings we experience some sort of loss. Even baby eagles have to be pushed out of the nest in order to experience the joy of soaring to even greater heights!

Wendy continued, 'There were still so many questions to be answered. I had got so used to my current lifestyle and routine. Would I be able to earn enough? And where would I live? What did I really want to do? I started digging deeper into what was really important to me in my work and career.'

'As more and more people began to hear about my situation, the more supported I felt. It was as if the universe opened up to answer all my questions and guide me towards opportunities that had been there all the time. So I stopped going to the hotel. I even enjoyed not going to work. I liked working within a different environment. Sure, I missed some of the people, but not the work, not the job and not those long, boring meetings and company politics. I was ready for something new!'

'It's been six months now and I've earned more money in that time than I would in a year at the hotel. It's not just about the money though. I look back and laugh as I now realise that what seemed like a barrier was actually an opportunity which has led me to be much happier and a lot more 'me' than I have ever been!'

Breaking Through

For Justine, the comfort zone was what she called her charmed life: married with three beautiful children, a successful, well paid job, flashy sports car, designer clothes, unlimited expenses, a gardener and housemaid, as well as exotic holidays! 'But beneath it all I was miserable and had been for several years. I was doing my best to stay in denial. Jumping ship after 25 years of married life and at this stage in my life was not a pleasant prospect. I tried everything I could to fix my misery – more clothes, expensive therapies, and another holiday - but nothing seemed to work. Something kept nagging at me that there was more to life than a cold, indifferent marriage and material trappings. What had I done in this life of which I could be proud? Where was the love in my life? What did I really want? I could think of nothing to satisfy the critic within. If I died tomorrow I would be missed by no one and forgotten by all. I felt like crying a river of tears. It wasn't fame and fortune I wanted. No! It was something less tangible but I knew I wasn't happy at all.'

'My journey to self-healing began around seven years ago, triggered by panic attacks, inertia when not working and a general malaise that affected my mood and will to live. Mid-life crisis hit me with full force and I could no longer ignore the signals from my body. I felt fat, silted up, physically and energetically, and totally depressed emotionally. I could no longer hold together the false impression of a healthy, successful and vivacious human being.'

'In my quest to improve my deteriorating physical, mental and emotional state I decided to do a complete detox from the inside out. After a brief stay in a health farm, I put myself on a strict vegetarian diet and cut out all liquids except water. The weight began to drop off at a steady 1 kilo a week. Within 9 months I had lost about 28 kilos. I remember saying to myself at the time 'This is Justine's diet for life!' My friends and family could not believe how different I looked and I was secretly delighted with my new body. However, I knew that it was not just about my body image. I wanted to remove all the stress in my life as well and I knew that included my high powered and well paid job. To the shock and dismay of my employers, I resigned. I had been plotting it for some time, but it was a huge leap of faith for me. First of all I would no longer have an independent income. Something I had always prided myself on. I had always valued my independence and hated asking anyone for money. I also liked the freedom of buying whatever I needed and looking good, which all costs money. Secondly, I would lose my status symbol and the one thing in my life that gave me respect. Last of all, I would have no excuse for spending time away from my family and would have to face my demons. My job was, after all, a huge diversion. A brick wall to the real issues I was avoiding in my life. That was the scariest thing of all – facing my demons.'

'I had no intention of returning to work, so the huge amount of free time I now had allowed me to indulge myself. I wanted to get in touch with myself and my emotions. I learned meditation and alternative therapies. I read copiously about self improvement and the mind-body-soul connection. I started a journal and wrote poetry. I was on a journey of self-realisation. I took myself out into the wilderness for about five years and re-discovered parts of me I always knew existed but had deliberately submerged. This was often painful and scary, but also liberating. During this period I became more of a recluse and I came to the conclusion that my marriage was doomed. I realised that to stay in the relationship was a sentence of death. We were both on a different journey and I needed to get started with mine.'

'I agonised over my decision to leave, worrying about the effect it would have on my children, the anger it might incur in my husband and the alienation of my friends. Last but not least, I worried about my ability to look after myself. I was never a greedy person, but I liked a respectable lifestyle and wasn't sure if I had the ability or the energy at the age of 47 to make a decent life for myself on my own.'

'After a few false starts – I tried to leave and then changed my mind, rushing back to what was safe and familiar, back to my comfort zone - I finally reached a level of despair that was far deeper than the fear of losing my children or material comforts. I woke up one morning and cried an ocean. I cried for what I had become, I cried for what I had denied myself, I cried for my family and I knew that even if I lost everything, I had to leave. Once I had made the decision, once I had surrendered to my truth, once I had decided what was really important to me, once I had faced my fear, my life opened up around me. I am not saying it was easy, but the huge pressure of living a lie, being someone I could no longer be, was lifted. It was a breakthrough and I was truly on my way to self realisation.'

Climbing Over

In Sarah's case, life was one big party and she loved it that way. 'My life was great... and then suddenly it wasn't. After a routine check-up at the doctors, I found myself in agony. Despite painkillers and rest, the pain in my back got progressively worse. I couldn't work, so I kept going back to the doctor who kept increasing the painkillers and exploring what it wasn't. I struggled to walk. Making a cup of tea was a real effort. Feeding myself reduced me to tears and shopping wasn't possible as I couldn't carry anything.'

'I lost my job, and had to move back to Cornwall to be looked after by my grandmother. I kept going to the doctor but all they could do was to eliminate what wasn't wrong with me. Appointments became the highlight of my week. A laparoscopy told me that my reproductive system was fine. A specialist told me that I didn't have IBS (irritable bowel syndrome) and a physiotherapist kept trying different treatments. I cried a lot. The pain was unbelievable and I went from hurting to agony and back again and I remember looking at all the boxes of painkillers and thinking that if I took them all then I wouldn't have to face another day of agony. Being assessed to qualify for incapacity benefit was humiliating, particularly since I had never experienced being unemployed, and to add further distress, I lost my apartment and was left with a huge debt of negative equity. The future did not look bright and I was firmly stuck behind a wall.'

'I didn't give up, kept looking at other options and eventually a light at the end of the tunnel appeared seven months later in the form of a chiropractor recommended by a friend of a friend. It's sometimes strange how the right people appear in your life at the right time. Looking at my x-rays, he could clearly see damage to my lower spine, while I cried with relief as he prescribed a series of treatments. I had intensive adjustments, wore a support belt, couldn't sit down for months, did gentle exercises and still took painkillers when I really had to. The summer was spent lying on the beach not being allowed to swim but watching others enjoying themselves. I decided to speed the recovery process along by focusing on what I could do and consequently spent 2 months making sugar flowers for a wedding cake whilst lying on the floor. I finished a patchwork quilt I had started as a child and I also learned to type. I attended a counselling course (and realised that we all have our issues!) along with an NVQ course on IT and twice a week I drove to St Austell to develop my NVQ Assessor qualification in catering. I couldn't cook anymore, but I could teach.'

'Two years later I qualified as an NVQ Assessor and began looking for work and was offered a job in London, training hotel receptionists on Front Desk Systems. I took it, learned it, excelled in it and was subsequently offered a posting overseas. I grabbed the opportunity and have never regretted it. In fact, if I hadn't spent two years of my life horizontal, I wouldn't be where I am and who I am today. Things happen for a reason and although it took years for me to discover what the reason was, I am glad it happened.'

"If your fascination with what you already have precludes you from creating what you don't have, you're likely to end up as an accident on the highway to the future. So strike a balance between continuity and innovation. You can't have one without the other; both are essential."
Ken Blanchard, Mission Possible

I'm often asked what brought me to live in the Middle East. Well, I decided to step out of my comfort zone, take massive action and change everything about my life!

I was 19 and he was seven years older than me, and extremely good looking! He came from a completely different background and when he told me he lived in a mobile home, I had a vision of a caravan in the middle of a field! At that time I lived in a huge house with my parents and I remember he later told me it was a daunting prospect walking up the long and impressive driveway to pick me up on our first date! We clubbed, partied, went off to Dorset on the weekends and since I had had few boyfriends before that time, I had no reference points of what to expect. In fact, looking back, I probably didn't appreciate all the little things he did do to make me feel special. It didn't matter because by then, I was totally in love with him. I adored him and set him up high on a pedestal. About a year into the relationship, he told me he was taking a year off work and travelling around Europe with a friend. My initial disappointment turned to delight when his friend dropped out and he asked me to go with him instead and what an amazing adventure it turned out to be! After six months of planning, we left Dover on May 15th 1980 and set sail for Jersey, to begin a two-year adventure around Europe with only £600 each in our pockets, a small Fiat 127 packed to the brim, and a tent. My mother was horrified at the prospect and thought me ill-equipped for life in a tent. Secretly she predicted I would be back within two weeks! Instead, I loved it! I loved the freedom to go where we wanted, whenever we wanted and I loved him. We were best friends and passionate lovers! This was probably one of the most incredible times of my life. New places to see, people to meet and all with the person you want to be with! In the UK, jealousy had often got the better of me and to the detriment of our relationship, but there was no need for me to be jealous now as we were together 24 hours a day, 7 days a week. I was in heaven!

Two years later, with a huge box of photos and a ton of memories that are with me to this day as souvenirs from this road trip, we finally returned to England. We each found suitable employment and a place to rent together. Another year passed and we bought a small house and that's when complacency set in! One night he came back late and admitted that he'd slept with someone else. I was devastated and asked him to leave immediately. In my model of the world, what he had done was unacceptable behaviour. In hindsight, I should have taken some responsibility for the situation and used it as an opportunity to talk and reconnect. I regretted this decision many times, as we continued to see each other for quite a number of years after but he would never move back in. It was always a volatile, rollercoaster-of-a-ride relationship and it's only on looking back I can appreciate the closeness and passion we shared and that I spent many subsequent years seeking in others. It was just after Christmas 1988, I was 28 years old having grown up through my 20's within this relationship, and again, my intuition instinctively knew he was seeing someone else. Although we had broken up before, something inside me also told me that it was different this time. That this was it. It's hard to put into words how devastated ......how broken.....how my world just disintegrated and fell apart....totally....and completely. Physically and emotionally I felt that my heart had been beaten, bruised and ripped apart. I cried. And cried. And cried. And cried even more. Months later things were pretty much the same and I was still crying. I kept going. Going to work. Going to dance classes. Going through the motions. It was as if I was on autopilot. But at home.....I just cried! The wall was around me and it was a very dark place indeed! Every day, it just got darker and the wall got higher. It felt like I'd been to the top of the mountain and been given a glimpse of paradise and then had it snatched away. And then I was forever trying to get back to the top again.

There comes a time when you have to make a decision. A decision is an opportunity to exercise your options and choices. And you have to make a choice: to stay within the confines of the wall; find a way through or climb over and move on! I decided to climb over and move on.

I started meditation with a group called the Brahma Kumaris. I would get up at 5.30am (friends will be shocked as I'm not known as a morning person!) and drive 45 minutes come rain, frost or shine to meditate with them in the morning. Then I would drive back home before the morning traffic to feed my cats, get ready and go to work. These were some of the kindest, purist people I have ever met. They never tried to pry or question my motives for attending their group. They just allowed me to be part of their community. It was like a safe haven for a time and it gave me a glimpse of light through the wall and that was when the wall started to crack!

It was also at that time that I decided this was really an opportunity to reinvent myself. I was noticing certain patterns of behaviour (and my mother had often said I was too bossy.....I prefer to call it assertive!) that often led me into trouble and confrontation with others. I started to look for opportunities overseas. I contacted everyone I knew overseas. There were auditions and job applications abroad and I remember asking my mother what else I could do after I mailed off yet another application form. I was feeling frustrated. I'd made a decision and wanted something to happen. Right now! She wisely told me that if I was absolutely sure that I'd done everything I could, that if I had left no stone unturned and taken as much action as possible, then I just had to wait for the universe to respond. And it did! Two opportunities appeared at the same time - one was in the Canary Islands, and the other one in Sharjah. At the time, I'd never even heard of Sharjah, part of the United Arab Emirates. Looking it up on the map, I decided there and then that if I didn't like it, I could always return home. And so a new journey of learning and discovery began!

"Until one is committed there is hesitancy, the chance to draw back.......always ineffectiveness. Concerning all acts of initiative (and creation), there is one elementary truth – the ignorance of which kills countless ideas and splendid plans; that the moment one commits oneself, providence moves too.

All sorts of things occur to help one that would otherwise never have occurred. A whole stream of events issued from the decision, raising in one's favour all manner of unforeseen incidents and meetings and material assistance which no man could have dreamed would have come his way.

Whatever you can do, or dream you can, begin it. Boldness has genius, power and magic in it. Begin it now."
Goethe

What are the walls that you are facing? What are the barriers blocking your way forward right now? And more importantly, are you ready to go on a journey of learning and discovery?

It's in the moments of our decisions that our destiny is made!

Only one potential successor approached the door and gave it a thorough examination. She tapped it and noticed its width and depth, pushing here and prodding there. Finally, she made a decision. She took a deep breath in.......and out, centred herself and then pulled gently on the door. Lo and behold, it swung open easily and effortlessly.

The ruler addressed the group. 'Success in life depends on certain key things. First, rely on all of your senses to fully understand the reality of what is going on around you. Second, I caution you against false assumption about what is possible and what is not possible. Third, be willing to make bold decisions and fourth, have the courage to act with boldness, courage and conviction. And finally, put your powers into action!

Is that wall really an obstacle or is it really a chance for you to learn and grow and learn how to deal with life in a more effective way? Or is it a challenge that makes reaching the goal that much more valuable

– because you had to strive for it? Or is it a lesson? The choice is yours. You can take all the things that looked liked obstacles and turn them into something useful and valuable to you.

Successful people make choices of how to approach the brick wall – tunnelling through, breaking through or climbing over – because they know that on the other side lies a garden of opportunity and the wall is an opportunity that helps you tap into your creativity and find new ways forward to get what you really want in life.

So what is the difference between successful people and unsuccessful people? *Successful people take action!*

Action causes a reaction but you've got to take action first! One of my friends is a fitness enthusiast. He subscribes to all the fitness magazines. In fact there is a pile of them stacked neatly in a corner of his lounge. He also has membership at an exclusive health club; however, the most exercise he gets is probably from lifting the health and fitness magazines from one corner of the lounge to the other. While he extols the virtues of a healthy lifestyle, talks about it, thinks about it and even reads about it, he does nothing! The first step is to make a decision and then back that decision up with massive action.

Just for a moment, close your eyes and imagine that you've completed the exercises in this book and have broken through your wall. How would you be feeling? What would you be seeing? How would you look? What opportunities would you have created for yourself and others? Would you be feeling happy, elated, excited or relieved? What sounds would you be hearing and what would other people be saying to you?

Just for a moment

The golden opportunity you are seeking is in yourself. It is not in your environment, it is not in luck or chance, or the help of others, it is in yourself alone. To get what you want, you change who you are, and you change who you are by simply changing the way you think and act!

So imagine it's your birthday and you can wish for whatever you want. What do you wish for?

'One ship sails east and another sails west
'Tis the set of the sail and not the gale
Which determines the way they go.
As the winds of the sea are the ways of fate,
As we voyage along through life,
'Tis the act of the soul that determines the goal,
And not the calm or the strife.'

Source unknown

CHAPTER 2

THE JOURNEY

THE JOURNEY

The other year, I had the opportunity to go to Sarawak, which is on the Malaysia side of Borneo. We were there to race in the Sarawak river regatta which dates back to the 1800's when all the different tribes used to gather together to race against each other in beautifully decorated longboats. Of course, back in the 1800's, some of the tribes were still cannibals so it was important to win the race or you had a good chance of being eaten! That wasn't going to happen to us, but you may still be wondering what I was doing racing in the Sarawak river regatta?

Until quite recently I had a segment on the local radio station called 'The Fitness Factory.' It was an opportunity for me to bring in a guest each week to talk about different aspects of health and fitness. One particular week, I had brought on a friend of mine who at that time, worked for an adventure company and we were talking about adventure holidays as a way to stay fit and healthy. She was also trying to get a team together from the UAE (United Arab Emirates) to go and race in the Sarawak River Regatta for the first time, so at the end of the interview, we announced the details over the airwaves to encourage registration. About a half hour after the show finished, my friend called me and asked myself and Jason, the DJ that I worked with, if we would like to go participate and cover the river regatta all expenses paid, courtesy of the Malaysia Tourist Board. Wow! If you're like me, you don't turn a free holiday down! But have you ever noticed that when you get offered something for free, there's usually some strings attached? And there were some strings attached to this 'free' holiday. We had to practice! Twice a week we would go down to the local creek to practice our rowing skills. This proved challenging as we didn't have a longboat. What we did have were oil drums, planks and ropes all strapped together...so nothing like a longboat! What also proved challenging was that we discovered that we had to get the rowing timing and intensity just right else we kept going round in circles or worse still, capsized! Quite a few practice sessions later, and having been tipped into the creek a few times as well, we finally mastered the art of rowing in one direction and at a good pace as well.

We arrived in Sarawak the day before the race and had time for one practice session in a longboat. Having got the weight evenly distributed and the timing and intensity perfected, we found ourselves moving swiftly along the Sarawak River and felt confident about our race which was due to start the next day at two in the afternoon.

Weather-wise, Sarawak enjoys wonderful weather most of the year and the following morning was no exception. I opened the curtains in my hotel room, looked out across the Sarawak River, and lo and behold, it was another beautiful day with longboats already out in full force.

At about 1.30pm I went down to the hotel lobby to meet the rest of our rowing team and we started making our way down to the jetty. Looking up at the sky, there were clouds forming and the sky appeared to get darker by the minute. By the time we got in our longboat the water was quite choppy and as we turned the boat around at the start line, we found ourselves knocking into other boats and the current moving us farther away and in the wrong direction from the finish line! So there we were, paddles poised and I looked at my watch. It was almost 2 o'clock. And you know what it's like...when you're waiting for something to happen?

Just waiting..............for something.............to happen...............! And YOU want something to happen! You've made a decision to move forward – to take the steering wheel rather than the back seat - and now it's up to you to make it happen! It can be challenging to keep going! But the journey of a thousand miles really does begin with the first step.

"We all start somewhere!"

So congratulations! You've taken that first step because you're reading this book right now!

We're going on a journey, your own adventure holiday, and in order to ensure its success, we need to prepare to make way for the new and for that, we need to let go of the old: old patterns of thinking and behaviour, old beliefs that no longer serve you, and clear some space.

In the Peruvian tradition to create space, they look to the energy of three different animals – the snake, the puma and the condor. The first animal is the snake which represents the first step of growing, gathering energy, shedding our skin as well as shedding the past and leaving old ideas behind. The Puma is the second animal and represents taking the energy that's released by leaving the past behind and applying it to this life and making this life beautiful right now and using that new-found energy to make your dreams and goals happen! The third animal, the condor, represents enlightenment and personal success so that we can soar to extraordinary heights.

In the Far East they use Feng Shui to ensure your energy is aligned with the environment so let's call this, Feng Shui for the mind! Alignment and balance is the core and essence of Feng Shui and it has both internal and external benefits. The two basic premises of Feng Shui are that 'man's state of mind and energy affects his environment for good or bad, and secondly, that the condition of the environment also affects our internal state.' What we want to create is a clear space both internally and externally to allow the new opportunities to enter by getting rid of the clutter. And tap into the snake energy to shed the past.

Feng Shui for the mind:-

1. Make a list of all the things that you are aware of right now that you have to do and set yourself a deadline for completing each item. Remember that everything that is incomplete drains energy away from what you really want to achieve.

2. Clean up your home and office inside and out. Remember, our external world is a complete mirror of our internal world, and vice versa. And here's a tip, you could get someone else to do this for you!

(By the way, I've just finished tidying out my car. I never knew you could fit so much into a glove compartment!)

3. Throw away everything you don't use or have not used for the last six months. I know, it's tempting to put it in a cupboard or in the loft and so I remind you that what is on the outside is a reflection of what is happening on the inside of you. And what happens when you do eventually open that cupboard or venture into the loft? That's right; it falls out all over the place!

4. Make a list of all the things you have started and not yet completed. This could be decorating, putting up some shelves, turning up the hem on a new pair of trousers or completing an important plan of action for a client. And then start completing them!

5. List all of the commitments and agreements you've made and not met. Commit to what you can fulfil and get rid of the ones you can't. I used to have a tendency to say 'yes' to everything and then try and wriggle out of it later. One particular incident was when I'd promised to do a personal training session at the gym with a friend. I felt terrible each time I came up with an excuse to cancel especially when my friend was so disappointed. I was letting my friend down as well as myself by going back on my word. Finally, I fulfilled my obligation and decided that I would have to be more careful about what I did commit to in the future!

6. Make a list of everyone who has borrowed from you or owes you and a list of all that you have borrowed and owe. (When I'm owed money and it does not seem to be coming to me freely, I sit back and think about where I may be withholding payment or check to see if I owe anyone any money. Money is an exchange of energy and if you're giving it begrudgingly it cannot flow swiftly and freely back to you). Set yourself a deadline for clearing the list.

Ultimately, *you* are the creator of your universe! You are the cause for all the effects in your life! This can be quite a concept to get your head around and it always provokes comment when we talk about it in our personal development programs. It may not necessarily be true, and what I can tell you is that when I do take full responsibility for what's going on in my life, I'm empowered; I have more control and more choice to do something about it! After all, if it's not your fault, how can you do anything about it?

One of my dear friends complains that she is continually dogged by bad luck. She is attractive, kind, generous to a fault, yet seems to go from one difficult situation to the next. Last year it was because of a bad tenant, this year it's a difficult landlord, before that it was her husband and then her manager. Of course, it's never her fault!

Just the other year it seemed that everything I turned my attention to, took one look at me and ran in the opposite direction! An important presentation didn't go as well as I'd envisioned. A sure-fire client never materialised. Carefully planned and orchestrated events took a nose-dive in the wrong direction. Equipment failed to turn up. It was easy to blame others – it always is – and admittedly, that can feel good for a short period of time. But you're still stuck! In fact, when something goes wrong and you can acknowledge it's your fault you should breathe a sigh of relief because that means you are in control. So knowing that 'I am the cause for all the effects in my life' I began asking myself questions to shift my stuck state. Rather than the 'why me?' questions, I started asking 'how have I created this situation?' And more importantly, 'what can I do differently to make this situation improve?' I then started to work with the answers that sprung to mind to change the situation and move towards what I really wanted.

Now, I don't know if we do create everything in our life, but accepting that we do puts us in a position of power over everything. *After all, if we create it then we can change it. If somebody or something else created it we are powerless to change it.* Listen to the people around you. Are they the creators of their universe or victims of circumstance? Are they interested in results or quick to give an excuse? Are they giving away their power to create the life they want by being at the effect of the economy, the environment, the government, their clients, their relationship, their age, or the business they are in? Of course, I know that you don't do that!

And are you ready to keep going when the going gets tough? John Stephen Akhvan kept going! Long after the crowd had left and the cameras moved away, a lone runner entered the stadium to complete the 26 mile marathon in the 1968 Mexico Olympics. Injured earlier in the race during a fall, he stumbled along more than one hour after all the others had finished. Hurling himself over the finish line, Akhvan of Tanzania finished last. But before you judge him as a loser, a victim of circumstance or unlucky, he said, 'My country did not send me 7000 miles to start the race. They sent me 7000 miles to finish it.' And finish it he did!

You are also the tour guide on this journey and you can choose the route you take. You can take time to stop and take in the sights on the way; evaluate the learnings and reaffirm where you are and where you want to be. I'm a firm believer that 'one size does not fit all,' (no matter how 'stretchy' the fabric!), and we all know that 'one diet does not work for everyone,' therefore we have provided you with a choice of three different ways to get to the other side of your wall. You can use just one way through, or a combination of all three or even create your own.

It's your wall

It's your journey

It's your choice of the way through

And you can choose the perfect way for you!

1. **Tunnelling** involves digging deeper to discover what drives you and motivates you to keep going when the going gets tough! You'll find out what's really important to you so you are totally aligned with what you want and have the rocket fuel to go get it!

2. In **Breakthrough** you'll discover that you have your own resident wizard within you. You'll discover how to give your wizard clear instructions to help you get what you want. You'll become aware of the fears and limiting beliefs that become dream stoppers and prevent you from getting what you want and experience how to break through those dream stoppers so that there is nothing holding you back.

3. As you are **Climbing Over** that wall you'll gain a deeper self-awareness about yourself and the other people you choose to surround yourself with on your stage of life. Looking in the mirror, you'll discover new ways to evaluate situations, events and relationships, to handle conflicts effectively and step back from emotionally charged situations to gain a deeper understanding of yourself and others.

And finally, once you've reached a 'garden of opportunity' you can start to identify your own success strategies so that you can recreate anything great you've done in the past right now and again and again in the future! You'll have the triggers to kick start your motivation strategy and understand which were the best decisions you made in the past, so you can use that same strategy right now!

> "You have powers that you never dreamed of. You can do things you never thought you could do. There are no limitations in what you can do except the limitations of your own mind."

Bang! The starter's gun fired at exactly the same moment as a clap of thunder shot through the clouds. Our paddles hit the water and we were off towards the finish line. The heavens opened; we were in the middle of a tropical thunder storm and out of the corner of my eye, I could see Jason, the DJ that I work with, giving a live commentary of the race. *Cheering each other on, we just kept going, rowing harder and faster, keeping the same timing and intensity. What I didn't tell you is that longboats are quite low to the water and with paddling, splashing and a tropical thunderstorm; they soon filled with water from both above and below. Other boats simply sank and we passed the heads of other team members just bobbing in the water as we kept rowing, focused only on the finish line. There were times when we were so tired, when the effort of continuing to paddle seemed too daunting; moments when the finish line appeared to be further away and we thought about giving up. But we kept cheering each other on; we kept going, focused only on the finish line and that sense of accomplishment and of 'really going for it.' We focused on what we really wanted. And we made it! Finally, we crossed the line looking like drowned rats! And it felt so good!*

You too can make it and now is the perfect time to choose the perfect way for you to make those transformations right now!

CHAPTER 3

TUNNELLING

TUNNELLING

At first, the mine superintendent thought he was the brunt of a practical joke. While making a routine check of the mine shaft at the end of the day, Frederick Wells caught the reflection of the setting sun glimmering and glittering off the wall. He rubbed his eyes and just couldn't believe what he saw. So he blinked a few more times before making a closer inspection. It was true. Right at the entrance of the mine shaft, right where everyone passed through on a daily basis he discovered a magnificent stone. Within hours, he found out that he had uncovered the largest diamond ever discovered!

At 3,106 carats, the gem was christened the 'Cullinan' diamond after Thomas Cullinan, the founder of the Premier Diamond Mining Co. in South Africa, where the stone was found. The gem was bought by the Transvaal government and was subsequently sent to England as a gift to Britain's King Edward VII, for his 66th birthday.

The security surrounding the transportation of the diamond was monumental. Armed guards escorted the carefully boxed gem by train to Capetown, and there they boarded a ship to Southampton, then proceeded by train to London, with final delivery to the vaults of the Bank of England. Photographers and newspaper men closely followed the shipment. What nobody, not even the guards, ever suspected, was that the gem in the box was a dummy. The real Cullinan diamond had been sent to London simply via registered mail.

The story doesn't end there! Cutting the huge, rough Cullinan was perhaps the greatest challenge ever facing a diamond cutter, and Joseph Asscher, the foremost diamond cutter of that time was entrusted with the task.

After two months of intense preparation and special tools being made for the cleaving and polishing, the stone was scrutinised and microscopically examined from every angle. The slightest miscalculation would result in this incredible stone shattering into a million pieces.

On February 10, 1908, with the King's representatives in attendance, notary publics to officially record the event, a doctor and two nurses in attendance, Asscher inserted a steel blade into the groove. The room was quiet. No one dared to breathe. You could hear a pin drop as he lifted the mallet. After what must have seemed like an eternity, he took a deep breath in and struck the blade sharply. It shattered. But the diamond didn't budge.

"Motivation is what gets you started!"

Are you ready to budge? Are you ready to make a shift? Are you ready to start mining the depths of yourself? Can you dig a little deeper to find out what's really driving you? Or maybe you feel like a prisoner ready to make your escape.

Katy thought she was ready to make her escape! She really wanted to get married and have children. She was in a relationship but her partner had made it quite clear that he was not ready to settle down, let alone consider children. On top of that, his family's religious values and beliefs made it unlikely that this relationship would ever end up in the marriage she so badly wanted. For the most part they got along well but every now and then, Katy's desire for a more permanent relationship and children would cause so much tension that she'd resolve to leave Ashok and move on. The first week apart was almost a relief, but usually halfway through the third week, she would miss him so much that she would convince herself that marriage and children were not so important. The making up and breaking up happened so often that amongst their friends it was something of a joke. In fact, they used to place bets on how long it would take Katy and Ashok to get back together again!

So often when we make a decision to step out of our comfort zone, the first thing we want to do is to run back to safety. It's like clearing out your wardrobe, your drawers or your filing cabinets; it tends to look worse for awhile before it gets better, and maybe you can even hear yourself say,

'I wish I hadn't started.' And so it is with 'tunnelling' and digging deeper. Do you think Madonna gives up when she gets a bad review? When the movie Swept Away got slaughtered by the press, she bounced back with a series of successful children's' books!

The challenge in going for what you really want does not lie in the obstacles that will often appear on your path, but in the temptation to stop, quit and accept a status quo. Fighting against this temptation is the greatest challenge that you will ever encounter on your way through the wall. When you are in complete control and stop considering quitting, you will be able to achieve total success.

Joseph had previously had a very successful consultancy with over 20 employees and a strong and respectable client base. Over the last few years employees had come and gone and so had the clients and while the business was ticking over nicely he wallowed in complacency. His life wasn't bad, but it wasn't brilliant either. While normally healthy, he didn't feel well and neither orthodox doctors nor complementary therapists could find a reason why. His last important relationship had been over a year ago and right now, he was just marking time and going round in circles. As a friend, Joseph has often been invited to our personal development programs. He has also been on our database for years, regularly receives program updates and information and has heard me talk about the extraordinary changes people go through during our programs, yet he had never attended a session or even talked about attending one! I was therefore delighted when a brief email landed in my email inbox which briefly stated 'count me in' for the next program. Joseph had made a decision! A decision to dig a little deeper and get through the wall of complacency.

Not only had he made a decision to join our NLP (neuro linguistic programming) Practitioner Certification Program, he had also made a decision to play at 150% and reclaim his power! He went through all the preliminary CD's and reading, and experienced the exercises as a person who's focused on results. The program certainly rocked his world and having discovered what was really important to him, he set some incredibly challenging goals. Not only that, in less than 3 months since completing the program he has achieved them all and more importantly, he's motivated, energised, feeling happier and healthier than he's been in a long time......and there's a spring in his step!

Both Joseph and Katy are interested in getting results. The difference is that Joseph is doing something about it and remaining focused on what he truly wants, acting as if he's already achieved it, and now knows what is truly important to him in order to feel happy and fulfilled. Meanwhile, Katy is still stuck behind the wall.

Are you still behind the wall, hoping that others will change, or that the world will come to you and someone else will be in the driver's seat? Are you just a passenger of life? Do you want to improve your results or do you just want to talk about it? Do you want to feel fulfilled and successful or just think about it? Because here's the thing, if you do nothing; nothing will happen! It's as simple as that! If you decide to find a new place to live or to buy a new car, that's great. You've decided what you want but you still don't have a new place to live or a new car to drive. You've got to call the real estate agents; you've got to visit the car showrooms. You've got to take action! Action causes a reaction!

Simon had been toying with the idea of pooling resources with a couple of friends and moving into a villa for more than a few weeks. 'We'd done the rounds – estate agents, classified ads, word of mouth – and seen a few good places too, but none of them quite fitted the bill. If the pool wasn't too small, parking was a problem; if we liked the rooms and fittings, the rent was too high.'

'That's when I decided to sit down and get really clear and specific about what we wanted and what was important to us all.'

'The wish list was impressive – 4 bedrooms with en-suite bathrooms, a nice kitchen, swimming pool and enough space to accommodate our 'family' which included, in addition to myself, the two girls, an 8-year-old son, a live in nanny-cum-maid, two cats, three dogs and a snake! My share of the rent, I decided, would be less than US$8500 per annum and the place would be located within easy walking distance of my office. As I closed my eyes, the goal floated out into my future time line, and decided to settle down just 20 days into the future!'

'My colleagues at the office laughed politely at my goal setting techniques; my cousin gave me the 'look' she reserves for what she likes to call my 'particularly mad moments.''

'We continued to take action and now we knew just what we were looking for. Two weeks later, we spotted the 'to let' sign on what seemed to be the ideal villa. It perfectly matched my wish-list; it had the 4 bedrooms, the kitchen, the swimming pool and lots of space. It even had a separate maid's room. What it didn't have, was a drawing room. I guess I forgot to put that on my list. Oops!

'We didn't let that stop us, though. We just went ahead and asked the landlord if he would allow us to construct a conservatory in front of the villa and he agreed. We signed the lease on day eighteen!

My cousin still refuses to believe this is the way it happened – she insists I must have already known about the villa before I drew up that wish list. Oh ye of little faith!'

"Action is a great restorer and builder of confidence. Perhaps the action you will take will be successful, perhaps different actions or adjustments will have to follow. But any action is better than no action at all."
Norman Vincent Peale

One of my friends is a consultant and says that there are four keys to success in everything that you do. The first thing is to know what you want and be clear about your objectives. The second key is to develop a feedback device that tells you whether what you're doing is moving you towards your objectives and goals or in the opposite direction. Now that would be useful, wouldn't it? The next step is to be willing to change your behaviour until you do start getting the results you want. How many times have you heard someone say 'I keep doing this again and again... and it's still not working!' If you keep doing what you've always done, you'll always get what you've always got! So do something different! Now!

My consultant friend was questioning a client to help him get really clear about his objectives when the client turned to him and said, 'Are you one of these consultants that's going to make me roll around on the floor or jump up and down like a crazy idiot?' My consultant friend smiled and thought for a moment before he responded. Then he said, 'No, I'm not one of those consultants, but if you could get the results that you want by rolling around on the floor and jumping up and down like a crazy idiot, would you be prepared to do it?'

'Hell no!' said the client. Needless to say, my consultant friend did not take on that client!

What would you be prepared to do in order to get the results that you want?

The results we get in life are driven by our actions; and our actions come about as a result of how we choose to behave. Our behaviour is driven by the skills and capabilities that we have.

My grandparents used to have a huge apple tree in their garden and occasionally my brother and I were allowed to pick the apples. We were also told not to eat the apples but 'breaking the rules' is one of the delights of childhood! That is until we bit into the apples, they were sour! Just suppose the apples in life are your results. And you want bigger apples, sweeter apples, and more apples? What would you do? That's right! Some of you would simply make your way to the local supermarket and buy more apples! But what really creates those apples? It's not the apples themselves; it's the seeds of our intentions, the seeds of our creativity that grow the roots that create the fruits! And so it is with the results we're getting in our life. If you want bigger results, better results, sweeter results, just focusing on the results alone does not create more results. We need to start digging a little bit deeper than that.

My company is in the business of human performance development which means that we help individuals and organisations improve their results. We're often called in to deliver service excellence programs, management and leadership programs or presentation skills. However, what we found was that just giving people the skills and abilities to do their job effectively does not always create a change in results. They also require the right attitude and a belief that they can improve their results. So our programs also focus on developing a 'can do' attitude and encouraging and installing a belief in each and every person that they can truly be good at what they do. Think of a belief like an on-off switch that drives your behaviour. Whether we believe we can or whether we believe we can't – we're probably right! Now we have people who have new skills and abilities, a positive 'can do' attitude and the belief that they can deliver service excellence or be a great leader or excel in presentations. Are we going to see a change in the results? Sometimes! But it's not enough because we need to go even deeper than that. We need to get to the roots. **If it's not *important*** for a person to be good at service excellence, leadership, presentations or whatever they do, **then nothing will change**. What are we talking about here? We're talking about your values!

Your values are what's important to you and they drive ALL your behaviour! They are your primary motivating force behind everything you do and also an evaluation filter that helps you decide whether your actions are good, bad, right or wrong.

Let me give you an example. Have you ever set a goal and achieved it? I suspect you said yes to that question. Have you ever set a goal and not achieved it? You probably answered yes again, so what's the difference between the goal that you achieved and the goal that you didn't achieve? Could it be that the goal that you didn't achieve would have been nice to achieve but it wasn't really important? Whereas the goal that you achieved was something that was really important to you. In other words, the goal you achieved was aligned with your values.

As motivational speaker Tony Robbins is fond of saying 'most people set themselves impotent goals.' And impotent goals are the ones that are not aligned with your values and what is important to you.

In business, motivating a team is one of the hardest challenges a manager faces. Why is it that the carrot will motivate one person while the stick motivates another? Think of that word 'motivation' like switching on a motor. The key that turns on the ignition of my car and the key that fits the ignition in your car are going to be completely different. Just try using my key to start your car. It's not going to work! And so it is with human beings. What's important and motivates one person may not be important and motivate another.

So what drives certain people? What drives Madonna to reinvent herself again and again, or at the age of 47 to go on tour again? What kept Nelson Mandela going, after all those years in prison to emerge as one of the most respected and impactful leaders of our time?

Trish, one of my mother's dear friends, is age 76 now and was and is very artistic in all ways. She's now unable to do most of the artistic endeavours that she used to undertake because of arthritis. What she does do is teach others to develop their artistic abilities and send articles to the Royal Horticultural Society. She also designs gardens. Her disability has not prevented her from doing what she loves most and what is important to her.

What drives you? What do you love the most?

> Where is my excitement?

> What interests me the most?

> What am I passionate about?

> What consumes my attention?

> What do I have the most energy for?

> What does my heart say?

Ask yourself

In his book, *The 8th Habit*, Dr Stephen Covey talks about three intelligences. The first intelligence is spiritual intelligence (SQ). He refers to this as 'ethos': your morals, ethics, code of conduct, your values. The second intelligence is EQ – emotional intelligence. EQ (or EI as it is often referred to) is about knowing how you and others feel at any given time, but more importantly, knowing what to do about it. It's your ability to communicate and empathise with others, and work together as a team. The third intelligence is IQ – your intellectual ability. An article by Master Trainer Robert Smith asks the question, 'In this age of knowledge and technology is a high IQ your key to success?' The answer is not necessarily. So what is the difference that makes the difference? Evidence shows that those who can influence, think out of the box, create and deliver a vision for themselves and others are today's winners. In other words, those with emotional and spiritual intelligence are today's star performers.

Harvard University did a survey of over 500 organisations including global companies, healthcare, academic institutions and government agencies. They looked at the competency models that each used to measure what made a successful profile for each job. The results fell into three categories: technical, cognitive and EQ skills. 'Technical' was defined as the skills to do the actual job, so for example, an accountant needed to have passed the necessary exams and requires a certain IQ to do this. Secondly, 'cognitive' skills measured analytical abilities. Finally, there was EQ which proved to be the difference that made all the difference. When the organisations were asked to name their star performers, EQ was the defining factor contributing to their success.

Dr. Covey says there is no point in having a high IQ if you do not have the ability to communicate and get along with others. On the other hand, there is little value being able to get along with others (EQ) if you have nothing to share. And ultimately, there is no value in having a high IQ or EQ if you are not working from a strong foundation of ethics. In other words, in order to be successful we require all 3 intelligences and it starts with SQ – your values, then EQ and finally IQ.

So where do your values come from? Your values are built up from your family, friends, religion, schooling, where you live in the world and its economics, and the media, to name a few areas. According to sociologist Morris Massey (author of The People Puzzle), if you want to know someone's beliefs and values, look at where they were when they were 10 years old, and what was going on in the world around them. That will give you a good idea about their beliefs and values. Maybe you've heard older people moaning about the youth today and saying, 'people just don't have any values anymore!' It's not that people don't have values, they are just different values. My grandmother was a child during the 1st world war and grew up with ration coupons. My brother and I always thought it strange when she used to butter the toast and then proceeded to scrape it off in order to make it stretch to a second piece! If you were brought up in the 60's the Beatles changed the face of music, colour television was introduced and the first man landed on the moon. If you were brought up in the 90's then it was all about globalisation, the personal computer, mobile phones and the Internet.

Morris Massey suggests that we go through a series of developmental periods that form and create our core values. First, the imprint period which is from birth to around age 7, the modelling period which is from age 8 to 13, and the socialisation period from age 14 to 21.

During the imprint period we are like walking sponges, literally soaking up everything that goes on around us, absorbing the beliefs and values of our parents, culture, religion and environment. We absorb and accept much of the beliefs and values of those closest to us without analysing or judging. As we move into the modelling period around age 8, we start finding role models and imitating and picking up some of their values and beliefs as we choose the people we want to be like. It's like trying on a new outfit to see if you like it or not. Role models could be a favourite teacher at school, a caring relative or a famous movie star. I still remember having a huge poster of pop star Marc Bolan on my wall, while other friends embraced pictures of Donny Osmond and David Cassidy!

'The first person I ever truly admired was my headmistress at school,' Sue told me. 'She was a fearsome character who commanded absolute respect and loyalty from everyone in the school. I was always in awe of her, but she used to talk in assembly about values and being the best that you can be, and that somehow has stayed with me ever since.'

For Terry, it was a fellow school teacher. 'He was the maths teacher but also trained and managed the school rugby team. His brothers were all famous athletes and he would have been too had he not been blinded in one eye. I admired him not only for his amazing athletic abilities, but also for the fact that he had re-modelled his career to get over his handicap. He was a strong character, and a family man with firm values of what was right and wrong. He made others excel and feel good about themselves and it was just good to be around him.'

'For as far back as I can remember, my 'role model' has been my mother,' Sandra told me. 'She is one of the strongest women I have ever come across and has managed to build a business empire, raise two children on her own, as well as be constantly surrounded by good friends and have an active social life. She has so much life in her – the mere fact of her walking into a room makes everyone want to be close to her, talk to her, and benefit from the glow of her smile.'

Who were some of your role models when you were growing up?

Who are some of your role models now?

As you move into your teenage years, the socialisation period, it's about spending more time outside of the family. This could be at a sports club, youth centre or becoming part of a gang and that may necessitate modifying or adapting your behaviour or values in order to fit in. I changed schools when I was 13, moving from a small private school of just 200 pupils to a large grammar school. It was a huge shift to fit in and become part of a new class, to join a different group of friends and get accepted into the netball team. It's this type of experience that can shape your values and defines what's really important to you now.

Some of you may remember the first Superman movie where Lois Lane turns to Superman and asks, 'What do you stand for?' Within a split second, he says 'Truth, and justice.' While his values may not be your values, he really knew what he stood for. Do you know what you stand for? What fuels your vision? Your values are why we do what we do! They are the energy and the reason to move forward. *Values are what matter to you and you take action in order to satisfy your values.*

One of the reasons I was so eager to pass my driving test was that it was important for me to have my freedom to get around rather than relying on other people for lifts or public transport. I made sure I passed my test first time!

Core values are those values that permeate most of what we do. They are what we move toward and away from. They are especially important because they are the key to understanding what we do and why we do it. Once you know your core values, your goals will begin to fall into place and you will have the energy to pursue them. Values are also context dependent, so for example, what's important to you in your career may be quite different to what's important to you in a relationship or in health and fitness. And remember, what's important to you may be completely different for others.

Jan was shocked when she was discussing marriage with her boyfriend. He said 'if you think I'm going to get married at 25 years of age and never sleep with another woman, you must be mad!' That's when Jan realised that fidelity was important to her in relationships. Oh, and she ditched the boyfriend!

If you have someone who has adventure as their number one value, are they going to enjoy the same kind of holiday as someone who has security as their number one value? Absolutely not!

Values tend to be the high level abstract words that mean different things to different people. In our programs I often ask students to pick a topic such as 'education' or 'sex' and then write down seven words that mean the same thing as education or sex to them as an individual. Next, I ask them to share their list with the rest of their group to see how many words they all have the same. It's surprising how rare it is even in groups of under ten people to find groups with the same words. Education and sex are universal experiences yet they both mean different things to different people.

Values control you on a day to day basis and they are what drive you toward what you want and away from what you don't want. Just for a moment, come up with a list of emotional states that you really want. I suspect you've got words like love, passion, happiness, security, peace, fun, freedom, adventure. Now come up with a list of emotional states that you want to avoid. This time, I suspect you've got words such as rejection, failure, guilt, feeling lonely, boredom, anger. Which would you want to avoid the most? And more importantly, what are you doing to avoid them?

Imagine a wooden plank laid out on the floor. If I offered you $1 dollar, would you walk across it? Of course you would; that's easy and safe!

What about if the plank was straddled between two chairs, would you walk the plank for $100 dollars? Probably yes, because there's not much danger if you do happen to fall off the plank. Now imagine that the same plank is stretched a 1000 feet up in the air across two tower blocks. The wind is blowing up a gale and the plank is sagging in the middle. Would you walk across it for $1000 dollars? It's getting tougher now, isn't it? And what if I offered you $1 million dollars to walk across a plank stretched across a deep ravine that will result in your death if you should fall? Would you be willing to take the risk? Of course not! Just for a moment, imagine that your dearest and closest friend is hanging from the middle of that plank 1000 feet above the ground? Would you be willing to walk across the plank in order to save your dearest and closest friend? It's not about the money now, is it? This is about what's really important to you.

So how do you find out what you stand for? How do you find out what's important to you and others? Like a movie, we don't see the film crew. It's the questions that help you get to the crew! So let's ask some questions!

Digging deeper:

1. Pick a context (for example career, relationships, family, health & fitness, personal growth or spirituality)

2. Think of what's important to you about your (work/relationships/ health etc.). Write down the things that are important to you about your (work/relationships/health etc.)

3. To help you get started, we've listed some values overleaf. Some of these values may be more important to you than others, or you may come up with others that are not listed.

Advancement	Honesty	Peace
Authenticity	Integrity	Power
Caring	Intellectual growth	Profitability
Contributing	Inspiration	Security
Effectiveness	Influence	Status
Fame	Joy	Success
Friendship	Justice	Tolerance
Freedom	Kindness	Truth
Happiness	Lawfulness	Wealth
Health	Love	Wisdom

4. Keep asking yourself the same question 'what's important to me about... until you have a list of at least 10 words or more.

5. Now find the top 8 and rewrite them according to their importance to you with 1 being the most important and 8 being the least important.

Ken Robinson, a leading guru on creativity tells the story of Gillian Lynne. You may have heard of her and you may not. She's a choreographer and if you haven't heard of Gillian, you've probably heard of some of the productions that she's been responsible for like Cats & Phantom of the Opera. When asked how she got to be a choreographer, she says it nearly didn't happen. When she was at school in the 1930's, she was a terrible student, always fidgeting and always giving her homework in late. While she was OK with this the school were not and so they sent a letter to her parents suggesting she see a psychologist. She sat on her hands during the appointment so she wouldn't fidget while her mother described all the problems. Gillian felt terrible. Not only was she being a problem, she was also causing problems for her parents too. After listening to her mother speak for about twenty minutes, the psychologist came over to Gillian and said he needed to speak with her mother alone and they left the room. As they turned to leave the room, he leaned over his desk and turned on the radio. Outside the room, the psychologist turned to Gillian's mother and said 'let's just stand and watch,' through a window. The minute they left the room, Gillian was on her feet moving. 'Mrs Lynne,' said the psychologist, 'Gillian isn't sick. She's a dancer! Take her to a dance school!' This was wonderful, says Gillian. 'It was filled with all the people who cannot sit still; people who have to move to think.' And that was what was important to Gillian! Gillian went on to have a career with the Royal Ballet and later set up her own school and has given pleasure to millions by being in her element, engaged, interested, passionate and excited by what she does.

Your values fuel *your* energy and passion, and help you find the things that really engage you. And if you want to motivate others or find out what's important to them, simply ask them *'what's important to you about...?'* You can use this in business to find the keys to motivate your team, in relationships with others, in sales and negotiation, coaching and counselling.

- Passion motivates – follow your bliss and the energy of enthusiasm will be with you

- Love motivates – let your heart lead and love will be your fuel

- Purpose motivates – know what you are here to do and do it!

- Pain motivates – let life's difficulties teach you, learn from your lessons and move on

- Competition motivates – if you like a challenge, compete with your own best by going for better than you have ever done before

- Ideas motivate – collect your ideas and let them develop and grow into projects and goals

- Imagined outcomes motivate – dream on, dream of greatness and dream a little bigger than you currently believe is possible

- Past experiences motivate – do it differently this time

- Truth motivates – know yourself and be true to yourself in everything you do

- Inspiration motivates – discover what it means to live an inspired life and live it

(Source unknown)

Some people believe that your values are with you forever, but the field of NLP (neuro linguistic programming) has a different view. After all, you only have to look back over your own life to understand that what was important to you at age 15 is different to what's important to you right now. A career change, a shift in your relationship, or the addition of children can have an instant and dramatic effect on what is important to you.

In our workshops we spend a couple of days on values, understanding the evolution of values based on the work of Dr Clare Graves, ensuring values alignment and checking for values conflicts. This helps you understand why you behave in a certain way in certain situations and change it if it's a problem. Remember that a lot of our values and beliefs came from our parents, culture and heritage during the imprint period, which means we probably didn't consciously choose them, so it may be unlikely that they are supporting all your goals now!

Keeping his emotions tightly in check, Asscher went through the painstaking motions once again. And this time, he was successful. The stone split exactly as he had planned and with further cleaving, sawing and polishing, the diamond produced nine major stones, 96 minor ones, and 10 carats of polished fragments. The largest, named Cullinan I, or 'The Great Star of Africa' is the largest cut diamond in existence and at 530 carats, it is a magnificent pear-shaped gem, set in the royal sceptre of the British Crown Jewels.

In every brick in your wall there awaits a diamond of opportunity to be discovered, and now that you've discovered what fuels your passion, it's time to break through any limiting beliefs that may be holding you back to getting what you really want!

CHAPTER 4

BREAKTHROUGH

BREAKTHROUGH

Do you remember that wonderful movie, The Wizard of Oz? Dorothy and her dog Toto find themselves transported over the rainbow to the Land of Oz where they quickly find out that they have angered the wicked witch of the West. Their only hope of getting back to Kansas is to seek the help of the Wizard of Oz and so off they skip down the yellow brick road towards the Emerald City. On her journey, Dorothy is joined by a scarecrow that can't make up his mind because he doesn't have a brain. In fact, he believes himself to be a failure because he can't even scare a crow. They next encounter and rescue a tin man whose chest is empty and he desperately seeks a heart, and finally a lion in desperate need of courage. All of them believe that the Wizard of Oz has the power to grant their wishes and on this adventure, successfully overcome frightening experiences to halt their progress by the wicked witch of the west. Finally, they reach the Emerald City and after much pleading they are granted an audience with the great Wizard of Oz. He agrees to grant their wishes but only if they can perform one more task – to bring him the broomstick of the wicked witch of the west.

> "Your chances of success in any undertaking can always be measured by your belief in yourself." - Robert Collier

Guess what? You have your own wizard residing within you and whatever is happening in your life right now is undoubtedly the result of the orders your Wizard receives and carries out. The wizard within is your unconscious mind.

We have a conscious mind and an unconscious mind (the latter is sometimes referred to as the subconscious mind). Think of the conscious mind like the rider of a horse, setting the direction, getting clear about where you want to go, and formulating your goals. It wouldn't be very useful asking a horse to do that for you, would it? The horse represents the unconscious mind that gets you to your objectives, goals and destination. So it's a partnership between your conscious and unconscious mind. When you first learn something you use the conscious part of your mind and back that experience up with your unconscious mind. Do you remember when you were first learning how to write? Everything was awkward and you had to think about every little movement of your pencil and your hand. Each line or curve had to be carefully controlled and in the right direction. It seemed impossible to produce straight lines and smooth curves, let alone produce letters on a line on a page. As you continued to practice, each experience was backed up in your unconscious mind so that now, you can write your name without even thinking! Isn't that great?

All of your learning, all of your behaviour and all change takes place in the unconscious mind. For example, if you want to move your arm, you may decide consciously to move your arm but you have to delegate the behaviour of moving your arm to your unconscious mind because there are 159 muscles between the tips of the fingers and the shoulder blades, so to move your arm consciously would probably take all day!

All of this means that if you want to learn anything new, behave differently or change, then it's the unconscious mind that does ALL that for you.

Is it too good to be true? It could be because what you think is what you get! Imagine that you had not learned to write as a child and as you grew up you had tried a few more times and failed. Not only would your unconscious make you relive that failure every time you picked up a pencil, but it would also give you rational reasons to give up, like 'you're not good enough,' 'how many times have you failed before,' 'what makes you think this time will be any different!' Does this sound familiar?

So let's find out what's going on inside.

Just for a moment, close your eyes and remember a recent and enjoyable experience. I suspect you are seeing pictures, hearing sounds, feeling feelings, smelling smells, tasting tastes or talking to yourself inside your head. Or a combination of those things. These are the six things that we can do inside our head at any given time. Of course, if you admitted that you talked to yourself thirty years ago, you'd probably be marched off to a mental institution but now it's acknowledged that we do, indeed, talk to ourselves inside our own head! And what is it that you are saying to yourself inside your head? Our external world is a complete mirror of our internal world, and vice versa. So what pictures are you creating inside your head right now, what are you hearing and thinking about? Are you thinking about what you want or are you thinking about what you don't want? Because here's the thing; *you can't think about what you don't want to think about without thinking about it!* You might want to read that last sentence again! If I were to say to you, 'whatever you do, don't think of a pink elephant!' What's the first thing that comes into your mind? That's right! A pink elephant, and yet I told you not to think of one! Our mind cannot process negatives, yet so often when I work with people they tell me what they don't want and then wonder why their life is such a complete mess. Have you ever said to yourself before an important meeting or appointment, 'I hope I don't mess this up'?' And what happens? You mess it up! Or just before a critical presentation, 'I hope I don't forget what I've got to say!' You guessed it! Your mind goes a complete blank! Or my favourite – when you're in a coffee shop with a friend and he leans over and says, 'don't look round now, but…' It's nearly impossible not to look round and have a peek! Your body is designed to produce behaviours based on what you think about, based on what you focus on and your unconscious is the most powerful part of your mind and is the very thing that can help you or hinder you.

Give this a go!

The other year, one of my friends asked me to help him prepare a presentation for an important interview. As we were preparing I also encouraged him to be positive, upbeat and recognise his talents and gifts but he kept saying 'I know I won't get it' over and over again. And guess what? He didn't!

Your unconscious mind runs your body and your life! Your conscious mind is responsible for approximately 10% of what you are aware of day to day. Your unconscious mind is responsible for the other 90% that you are most often not aware of. And your unconscious mind believes all of your negative mind-chatter!

> "An obvious fact about negative feeling is often overlooked. They are caused by us, not by external happenings. An outside event presents the challenge but we react to it. So we must attend to the way we take things – not to the things themselves."
> Vernon Howard

According to research we have over 60,000 thoughts each day and most of those thoughts are the same ones repeated over and over again. You know this is true. Just remember a situation that was causing you some stress. Chances are you went over it time and time again. Are your thoughts helping you or sabotaging you? Leading behavioural researchers have found that as much as 77% of everything we think is negative and counterproductive and conspires to work against us.

We also receive a lot of negative 'programming' from the outside world. For example, if you grew up in a reasonably positive home, you probably heard the word 'no' more than 150,000 times. 'No, you can't have that!' 'No, don't touch that!' 'No, you mustn't eat that!' This unintentional negative programming can have a lasting effect on your life! The other day, I was in the supermarket when I heard a loud voice boom out, 'I have told you a thousand times, if you're coming shopping with me you must stay by my side.' The words were harmless but the voice was sharp. The next phrase from the same mouth can only be described as devastating: 'You will never amount to anything!' I silently cringed.

In the previous section – Tunnelling – you read about the Imprint Period between 0 – 7 years of age. Like a walking sponge we soak up the values, beliefs and attitudes of those around us. Imagine the effect on a child if he is repeatedly told that he is worthless, stupid and will never amount to anything. On the other hand, imagine the effect on a child if he is repeatedly given praise and encouragement. Perhaps you want to think back to your own childhood and consider the 'programming' you received from those around you?

A pat on the back!

Maybe you want to consider praising and congratulating yourself right now on the successes you've already achieved in life!

Remember, **your unconscious mind only reacts to what you feed it**. So YOU control the power of your mind and it is therefore up to you whether you use it constructively or destructively.

How can we use our unconscious mind constructively to get what we really want and to find new ways to break through the wall? First we need to be really clear about what we do want. The reason we need to be clear is that our focus influences a greater reality. Princeton University have been doing studies for over thirty years proving this very fact and have now conducted over 5 million experiments. People were called in to see what influence they had over a machine. Researchers were also interested to find out if there was any particular type of person that was better at this. And there was! Was it those who had psychic abilities, or strong willpower, maybe lots of confidence in their abilities? No! They found that people in love were the best able to influence a machine. Another research project was done in France by René Peoch. He used baby chicks in his experiments. As soon as they were born, a moveable robot was imprinted on the baby chicks to act as their mother. The robot was then placed outside the chicks' cage and allowed to move freely as Peoch tracked its path. After a time, the evidence was clear – the robot was moving towards the chicks more than it would do if it were wandering randomly. The desire and focus of the chicks to be near their mother was an inferred intention that appeared to have an effect on the machine.

What does this all mean? It means a person who has more joy, more love, more passion and who can focus has the most ability to create the life they want. Just for a moment think back to a time when you were totally in love or passionate about what you were doing. It's as if everything else – any outside noises or disturbances – just disappeared. What's that saying, 'time flies when you're having fun!' That's focus! What a great excuse to get more love, joy and passion in your life right now!

One of my students shared that a major influence on her life was Paramahansa Yogananda (Autobiography of a Yogi). 'I was totally impressed by his devotion and dedication to spirituality and his book was my introduction to self-realisation. I always dreamed that I would one day visit the ashram where he lived and low and behold I did just that. I spent three days in the retreat at Encinitas, California and I was totally thrilled to be in the same place where he wrote most of his books. It proved to me that if you feel passionately about something and really want it – you can manifest it!'

Who are some of the most successful people that you admire? Mahatma Gandhi? Richard Branson? Oprah Winfrey? Anthony Robbins? Mother Teresa? Lance Armstrong? What do all these people have in common? That's right – a passion for what they do!

Are you passionate about what you really want?

Imagine you have just been told that you won the lottery. How would you feel? Fantastic? Excited? Elated? Overjoyed? Just thinking about it right now has probably produced an effect in your body. It's like thinking about slicing a lemon in half and biting into it – it immediately makes your mouth water.

Here's an experiment you can try. Ask a partner to stretch their right arm out in front of them and think of words such as 'joy and happiness' over and over again or bring to mind a joyful experience. As they do that, try to push down on their right arm and you'll probably find their arm really strong and you come across lots of resistance. Now ask the same partner to continue to stretch their right arm out in front of them, but this time to think of the words 'depressed and sad' or recall an unhappy event or situation. As they do that, push down on their right arm and you'll probably find little resistance and their arm will be easy to push down. Your thought processes have created a reaction in your body.

Give this a go!

Have you ever noticed that when you're feeling really good about yourself everything seems to go so much better? Yet when you're feeling down in the dumps, nothing goes right. If you think you're going to mess up your presentation then chances are you will. On the other hand, if you choose to imagine a successful outcome, and psych yourself up for achieving, the chances are you will. How can you put yourself into a peak state instantly? Simply change your thoughts! How do you feel when you go to the office on a Monday morning after a terrible weekend? Depressed, that's right. And you feel even worse by the time you've finished telling everyone in the office just how bad it was! Stop, right now! What you think and focus on is what you get! How about turning your thoughts to all the good times, happy experiences and funny moments you've enjoyed? I still remember an afternoon spent with one of my good friends, Suzie, over twenty years ago. She was feeling sick so

I went round to keep her company and we ended up rolling around with laughter as we watched 'The Party' with Peter Sellers. She felt a lot better after laughing so hard and just the thought of that movie reminds me of that afternoon with Suzie and I immediately start to laugh now!

Remember, feelings are not something we have;
they are something that we do!

What about all the times that you've felt motivated, confident and energised? The time you got that job that you really wanted, when you were asked out by someone special or knew all the answers upside down and backwards on the test paper and just knew you would breeze through with honours! Would it be useful to be able to tap into all those feelings so you can use them anytime, anyplace and anywhere?

Give this a go!

Achievement accelerator. Write down a list of all the times in your life that you've felt motivated, confident, excited and really going for it! Think of these moments like eating a ripe, juicy strawberry (or your favourite chocolate). You can use these experiences to bring both your body and mind back to a motivated state in an instant. You'll have your own strawberry moments!

And it's much better to focus on what you want when you're feeling really good about yourself, isn't it?

Yes You! Give this a go as well

Do you want another way to instantly feel great? Then stand up right now and tense the muscles in your legs, hips, abdominals and across your chest. Standing up really straight with your shoulders back, look up and put a massive grin on your face. You know, one of those ones with teeth. Inside your head with your body tense, looking up and with a huge grin on your face, say 'yes, yes, yes, yes' over and over again in your head and try, really try and get depressed. That's right, you can't do it. You changed your physiology and jammed up your thoughts so it's just not possible to feel bad. You may get some strange looks if you do that just before you step into an important meeting, but even a subtle shift in your posture can affect how you feel. How would you be sitting right now if you were really excited and motivated? How would you be sitting if you were really confident? Make that shift right now and stay that way until you've finished reading this book!

When we start to focus on what we really want, there is an inherent potentiality of *not* being okay with *not* having that. In other words, when we decide on what we do want, we often start focusing on 'what would happen if we didn't get what we wanted' or 'what could go wrong,' and now we find that all our fears and limiting beliefs come up to the surface.

Think of all your limiting beliefs and fears as oil in a bowl, lying at the bottom, still and undisturbed. Along comes a goal and then it's like pouring water onto the oil. What happens when you pour water onto oil? It brings the oil to the surface and into conscious awareness. The oil represents all of our repressed emotions and fears and that means our passion and enthusiasm gets locked up in the oil.

Emma was 17 and had still never been asked out on a date and was convinced it was because she was overweight. She decided to go to Weight Watchers to lose the weight with the ultimate objective being to get a boyfriend. *And then the oil came to the surface.* What if she lost weight and still didn't get a boyfriend?

Desperate to stop smoking, Ian had heard about a book that was purported to be the miracle cure and guaranteed to help any reader permanently stop smoking. He was convinced that he had to get hold of this book. *And then the oil came to the surface.* What if he read the book and it didn't work for him? He would then feel like a complete failure!

I remember registering for Fire Walking Trainer's Training. As usual I left it to the last minute to book, and was disappointed that I would also have to go through the initiation training as well. I had already walked over burning hot coals so figured I could skip that part. It turned out that it was a pre-requisite to attending the trainers' training and I was impressed when Peggy Dylan, the founder of Sundoor, and often referred to as the mother of the western fire walking movement, personally responded to my email. So I booked the week at Le Cornu, in France.

I regularly attend personal development programs not only to upgrade my own skills but because I believe as a human performance consultant I should be 'walking the talk' and also be a delegate. Not only that, for the most part, I thoroughly enjoy these programs and most of my friends refer to me as a 'course junkie!' I laughed and joked with a close friend as I said that since Fire Walking Initiation was in the French mountains I hoped it wasn't one of those all-hugging-all-singing-all-crying courses! After all, I was used to sitting and taking notes, and taking in a much as possible on the types of courses I attended.

Talk about focusing on what you don't want! It turned out to be a self-fulfilling prophecy! Within a few short hours everyone was hugging, singing or crying. All my worst fears were slap bang in front of me ready to be dealt with! On top of that, I was probably the only native English speaker there amongst a group dominated by Germans and German speaking Swiss, with the exception of Peggy herself. I was sharing a room with 3 of them, one of whom happened to be a prolific snorer, and for a person who is keen on her privacy in the bathroom, it was communal showers all round! I was horrified! Thankfully, there was one private shower and since the Germans appeared to enjoy a sort of communal joie de vivre whether in or out of the shower, I silently thanked my lucky stars that the private shower was always vacant! The challenge of the fire walk paled into the distance when they next announced a naked sweat lodge – and a very cramped sweat lodge it was indeed. British to the bitter end, and stubborn, I was the only one decked out in a bikini and sarong!

> "Our deepest fear is not that we are inadequate. Our deepest fear is that we are powerful beyond measure. It is our light, not our darkness that most frightens us. We ask ourselves, 'who am I to be brilliant, gorgeous, talented and fabulous?' Actually, who are you not to be? As we're liberated from our own fear, our presence automatically liberates others."
> **Marianne Williamson**

Reading this you're probably wondering why I stayed for the full duration, went on to Trainers' Training and was subsequently honoured to be invited to the Masters Training. Admittedly, the retreat at Le Cornu is some distance from public transport of any kind so it would have been hard, but not impossible, to make an escape. In truth, it did cross my mind! But the course pushed me waaaaay beyond my comfort zone and proved to be one of the most profound programs I had attended in a long time and helped me re-connect to my heart. Peggy is an inspiring teacher and I also met one of my now dear friends, Helene, on this course. And at the end of the course…yes, you guessed it, I was singing and hugging along with the best of them!

What's the oil on your dreams and goals? Remember that everything you tell yourself about yourself becomes a direct instruction to your unconscious mind, so any time you make a statement about yourself that is negative in some way; you are actually directing your unconscious mind to make you become that person. The oil literally becomes a **dream stopper!**

Think about this

Some typical dream stopper statements could be:

- I'm not good enough

- I can't make enough money

- I don't have enough time

- I'm too old (or too young)

- I won't be loved

- I'm not good with figures

- It's too complicated for me to understand

- I'm not athletic

- I'm not good at relationships

- Exercise is hard

- I can't dance

- I know it won't work

Do any of these sound familiar? Let me tell you that these are just thoughts, they are not real. You cannot believe everything you think. They are just thoughts and have no power over you unless you choose to allow them to have power.

> Alice laughed: "There's no use trying," she said.
> "One can't believe impossible things."
> "I daresay you haven't had much practice," said the Queen.
> "When I was younger, I always did it for half an hour a day.
> Why, sometimes I've believed as many as six impossible things before breakfast."
> **Lewis Carroll, Alice's Adventures in Wonderland**

Dream stoppers are really just excuses! Ruth desperately wants to 'break through the wall!' She hates her job and is just clocking in and clocking out until she can leave. She may have to move out of her apartment if a suitable room-mate doesn't appear soon, and her boyfriend recently broke up with her. She has seen a number of fortune tellers who all tell her she needs to make a switch in all areas of her life and even recommended that she attend a personal development program in order to review and refocus. For over a year, she's been threatening to attend such a program but she has a wonderful excuse: she can't afford it! And she never will because she can use this as a wonderful excuse for never doing anything to break through to the garden of opportunity! I can't afford to move apartment, I can't afford to leave my job, I can't afford to get help! If all the parents out there waited until they could afford to have children, well none of us would even exist! And the thing about limiting beliefs is that the longer you hold onto them they become a self-fulfilling prophecy. If you believe you can't make enough money, you're probably not going to take the appropriate action and activate all your potential to make money. Then, when you don't make enough money, you can turn round and say, 'I told you I couldn't make money!' As human beings, we have a need to prove ourselves right and that just makes the limiting belief stronger and stronger.

If I were to ask you **'how heavy is a glass of water,'** you might say anywhere from 20g to 500g. Actually, the weight doesn't matter. It depends how long you try to hold it. If you hold the glass of water for a minute, that's not a problem. If you hold it for an hour, I suspect your arm will be aching. If you hold it for a day, then you may need to call an ambulance! In each case, the longer you hold it, the heavier it becomes and so it is with our limiting beliefs (or dream stoppers as I like to call them) – the oil on our dreams. Sooner or later the burden becomes increasingly debilitating and we won't be able to carry on.

Dream stoppers are limiting because when you believe something your mind is closed and deletes information that could challenge the dream stopper. You literally do not see, hear, or feel the exceptions.

David admits he was a cynical journalist who came along to one of our introductory programs expecting a 'load of new-agey nonsense!' 'I realised that it isn't what you think; it's how you think and since then have gone on to make massive changes in my life..........and they're still ongoing!'

Imagine how your life would change if you lived in an open state of awareness where anything is possible. This is a world without the shackles of dream stoppers.

We regularly incorporate fire walks, arrows breaks and board breaks into our personal development programs. We do this, not because the world has an urgent need for more firewalkers, arrow breakers or board breakers, but because the world does have an urgent need for people who can face their fears with courage and conviction. And I've seen these events inspire this sort of courage in others. It does something to the human psyche that helps us overcome our fears and limiting beliefs, and for many it's also the most exhilarating experience of their lives. As a consequence, it leads them to break through old patterns of behaviour and achieve incredible success in all areas of their life. I know my motive in doing my first fire walk was to simply start the year by being 'more than I thought I could be' and that if there were some curveballs, challenges and obstacles ahead I could overcome them with courage!

So what are these wonderful ways that we can loosen the dream stoppers that individuals have built up around their 'problems'? Often, I'll have a client come to me with a statement such as, 'I can't lose weight because I don't have any willpower.' This is a dramatic statement and demonstrates a great deal about their model of the world around weight loss. On their reality map, the city of Weight Loss has a wall around it that won't allow in willpower. It also implies that if willpower were able to penetrate the walls of weight loss, then losing weight would be possible. This is the map of their dream stopper. Is it 'true'? They certainly seem to be behaving as though it were true. And what is a dream stopper anyway? **A dream stopper is a feeling of CERTAINTY about something, that you KNOW where the line between problem and non-problem is, and it is exactly that feeling of certainty that gives us such conviction about our dream stoppers.** There are certain questions that are useful to consider and can take you through all the possible outcomes of your present dream stopper. For example:

Dream stopper: I can't lose weight because I don't have any willpower

What would happen if you lost weight without willpower?

What would happen if you stay the same weight even with willpower?

What would happen if you lost the weight with willpower?

What would happen if you stay the same weight without willpower?

What wouldn't happen if you lost weight without willpower?

What wouldn't happen if you stay the same weight even with willpower?

These questions act like a **Truth Box** and will help you to begin to examine the limits of your dream stoppers. The Truth Box will help you challenge your dream stoppers. Are they really true or just a convenient excuse that stops you achieving what you really want?

So are you ready to break through those dream stoppers that are holding you back from getting what you truly want? Are you ready to examine the limits of your Dream Stoppers using the Truth Box? Of course, you can stay right where you are, in your comfort zone, doing the same thing, every day, every week, every month and every year. And when your life hasn't turned out quite the way you wanted in five years, or ten years, or even 25 years, what will you be saying to yourself? Will you regret the things you did do, or regret all things that you didn't do? What is important is for you to start thinking differently about what you can do.

'You have powers that you never dreamed of. You can do things you never thought you could do. There are no limitations in what you can do except the limitations of your own mind.'

Catch the dream stoppers!

1. What specifically do you want? Be as specific as possible and write it down.

(If it's difficult to decide what you do want, then first make a list of what you don't want. Remember, we have more reference points for what we don't want. Next, go through the list of what you don't want and ask yourself, 'What do I want instead?' For example, I don't want to be poor. What do you want instead? I want financial freedom. Or 'I don't want to be overweight.' Ask yourself, 'what do you want instead?' 'I want to be fit and healthy.' Do you get the idea?)

2. Pick the four most important goals for you this year and write them down (and make sure they are toward what you want) and in the present tense.

* **VERY IMPORTANT POINT!** If you set a goal of 'wanting a new job by the end of the year' chances are that by the end of the year you'll still be 'wanting' a new job, because you've set the goal as 'wanting' and not 'having!' It would be much better to re-set the goal as 'I have a new job by (insert date)' and be as specific as possible about the job – type of job, salary, location, type of people etc.

3. **Dream stoppers!** Pick the first goal and ask yourself what are your dream stoppers holding you back from getting what you want? (eg. I can't afford it, I'm not good enough, I'm not attractive etc). Make sure you do the same for your other three most important goals.

4. The **Truth Box**. Take each dream stopper and run it through the 4 questions in the Truth Box and notice how you feel differently afterwards:

- What would happen if you did/could/were?

- What would happen if you didn't/couldn't/were not?

- What wouldn't happen if you did/could/were?

- What wouldn't happen if you didn't/couldn't/were not

Remember, life experiences, our culture, values, memories and decisions we have made in the past have all formed our approach to situations. We've developed a comfortable way to do things. It's natural that when we try new things all our fears, anxieties and dream stoppers come to the surface and it's important to break through them in order to change our results.

If you've ever been to Cairo in Egypt, you'll know that you can hire a horse to ride and take you around the pyramids. It doesn't matter whether you've ridden a horse before or not, because these horses have taken the same route for weeks, months and years and they will simply continue on the same route all the way back to the stables whether you fall off or not! If you decide to take a different route around the pyramids, you'll have to hold the reigns really tight in order to steer the horse in a new direction. Relax your grip for just a moment and the horse will go back to the old route, so you'll need to pay attention to ensure that the horse takes the new route. **Are you ready to steer your horse in a new direction?**

When my mother and father were courting they both loved competitive dancing. This was interrupted when my father left for Libya as part of his National Service and my mother caught polio. 'I never for one moment realised or even believed that I might never walk properly again,' my mother told me. 'On the one hand I had some wonderful friends who helped me all the way. What I never realised or expected was that it was going to be so agonising training muscles and nerves again. At night I would literally be screaming with pain and at one point I begged for my legs to be removed. However, my beliefs were strong and the next day, I would be 'at it' again training my muscles and nerves, and when your father finally returned from National Services, I walked down the aisle unaided!'

Your external world is a complete mirror of your internal world and by paying attention to what you want you can begin to erase the old negative and counter-productive dream stoppers and replace them with healthy, new, positive beliefs about yourself and the world around you. You can literally break through the wall to a garden of opportunity!

Captured by the wicked witch of the West, the Scarecrow, Tin Man and the Lion secure Dorothy's rescue and release, and return to the Wizard of Oz in order for him to fulfil his promise: brains for the Scarecrow, a heart for the Tin Man and courage for the Lion. As it turns out, the wizard is a good man, but a bad wizard. He's a good man in that he has the power to engender belief in others. All of them had demonstrated brains, heart and courage but it was the wizard who had the power to engender that belief in them. He awarded the Scarecrow a THD – Doctor of Thinkology, the Lion received a medal for his courage and the Tin Man a heart shaped clock for good deeds done. As for Dorothy, she realised that she had the power to help herself and had that power all along. 'If I ever go looking for my heart's desire, it's in my own backyard.' In other words, all the brains, heart and courage lie within you.

Remember you have your own resident wizard within and she can help you right now.

CHAPTER 5

CLIMBING OVER

CLIMBING OVER

One of my favourite books is called Illusions by Richard Bach. It's about the adventures of a reluctant messiah and at the beginning of the book there is a short story about some creatures that live at the bottom of a river bed. These creatures cling to the rocks as the river washes over them. It doesn't matter whether they are young, old or middle aged, they just cling to the rock and that's all they do for their whole lives! One day, one of the creatures pipes up and says 'I'm going to let go!' 'I'm just going to let go and see where the river takes me!' The other creatures were horrified and said, 'You can't do that. You don't know where the current will take you. It could knock you against other rocks, or scrape you along the bottom of the river bed. Besides which, you don't know where you'll end up.' But the little creature looked at them all and said 'I don't care. Because if I stay clinging to these rocks any longer, I'll die of boredom!'

Have you ever felt you were swimming, but not actually getting anywhere? Or that the current was dragging you back down? Have you ever wondered if 'this is it?' Have you ever wondered if there might be something more if you just dared to be different, stepped out of your usual routine or peeked over the wall to see if the grass really is greener on the other side?'

> "Change the way you see the world,
> and change the world."

In 1906, Italian economist Vilfredo Pareto created a mathematical formula to describe the unequal distribution of wealth in his country, observing that twenty percent of the people owned eighty percent of the wealth. The value of the Pareto Principle is that it acts as a reminder to focus on the 20 percent that matters. In sales, 80% of your business will most likely come from 20% of your clients, so you should put the most effort toward the 20% that gives you most of your business. In organisations, 20% of the employees will probably be doing 80% of the work. Therefore we should be recognising and rewarding those 20%. And in life, 20% of life is made up of what happens to you; 80% is determined by how you choose to react to what happens to you. That means that we really have no control over 20% of what happens to us. For example, we have no control if the traffic light is red or green. We have no control if the traffic makes you late which throws your whole schedule off. However, we can control how we choose to react to the red light or the traffic! Let's say you meet a friend for lunch and she knocks her cappuccino all over your business suit. You have no control over what just happened! What happens next will be determined by how you choose to react! You shout and proceed to get angry at your friend for being so clumsy and knocking her cup of coffee over. After all, she should have been more careful. Your friend apologises but you don't let up and she bursts into tears. You storm off in a bid to rush home and get changed for an afternoon meeting. You drive at breakneck speed, narrowly missing a truck as you run a red light. When you've changed and got back in your car to head to your meeting, you realise you've left your briefcase at the coffee shop. You finally get to the meeting 30 minutes late and it doesn't go well. In fact, as the afternoon continues, it progressively goes from bad to worse.

Why did you have a bad afternoon?

    a. Did the cappuccino cause it?
    b. Did your friend cause it?
    c. Did the red traffic light cause it?
    d. Did you cause it?

Of course, the answer is d, because of how you chose to react. You had no control over what happened at the coffee shop. How you reacted immediately after the cappuccino was spilt is what caused your bad afternoon.

Let me give you another scenario; you meet your friend for lunch and she spills her cappuccino all over your suit. While I suspect you probably wouldn't lean over and thank her, you could tell her 'it's OK,' it was obviously an accident and she should be more careful next time. The waiter brings you a towel and you get your things together to go home and change. You also call your next appointment to let them know you may be a few minutes late, thereby arriving calm, cool and looking fresh. The meeting goes well and you enjoy the rest of your day.

Two different scenarios; both started the same. Both ended differently. Why? Because you chose how you reacted! You chose how you responded to an experience and created a completely different result.

We can choose the way we experience an event or situation to create a completely different result. You can choose to see the glass as half full, or half empty. And why is it that some people choose to see the glass as half full, and others view it as half empty?

Maybe you've had the experience of going to a party with a couple of friends. When you call the next day, one friend says that the party was brilliant, while the other has a completely different, and less than favourable opinion. Why does that happen?

Let me explain what's going on inside your head. It's estimated that we take in over 2 million messages of sensory awareness at any given moment through our five senses - seeing, hearing, feeling, smelling and tasting. According to research, we can only consciously be aware of 7, plus or minus 2 pieces of information (and for some of us it may be even less than that!) and we run the additional information through a set of filters. We all filter information differently. Our filters are like a point of view, and are built up through our life experiences. Family, peers, schooling and education, culture, religion, politics, beliefs, wealth, physiology, memories, decisions, values, attitudes and even our language all affect how we filter information. These experiences and influences create our filters for us and they colour how we view the world. Just look at other people around you right now. Everyone around you has had different life experiences, has different memories and has made different decisions. That means that they filter information differently to you and the way that you experience the world and the way that they experience the world is also going to be different. No wonder it's sometimes so difficult to get along with the people you live and work with every day!

Think of it like wearing a colour tinted lens on a pair of sunglasses. The tint on your lens is going to be slightly different from everyone else's, **so the way that you experience the world and the way another person experiences the world is going to be different.**

Do you see the face of a Native American.... or an Eskimo.....or both? The object lesson here is that most of us communicate with others expecting them to have the same experience as ourselves!

On a recent program, Karim shared with me that 'Filtering information and the concept of viewing information in a different perspective to the person next to me has helped me communicate better with people, or at least be more tolerant (I like to think!!).'

Give this a go!

Our filters create our interpretation of the world around us and how we choose to interact and interpret the world's interaction with us. Think of it like a projection, a ray of light from a projector. Whatever colour of light is projected on the screen alters the image on the screen. Just for a moment, try this experiment; close your eyes and inside your head repeat the word 'blue' and keep repeating the word, 'blue, blue, blue..........' Do this for approximately 20 seconds. Now open your eyes, look around, and you may notice the world looks a little bluer, or you may find that your eyes are drawn to and pick out everything that's blue immediately. What you've done is project a blue light and there will be a blue tint to your map of the world. Project a green light and there will be a green tint to your map of the world.

So the way we choose to experience the world is dependent on how we filter and then how we project those experiences. Do you project and perceive life as a problem to be solved or as a mystery to be enjoyed?

You may have heard the old Chinese Taoist story of a farmer in a poor country village. He was considered wealthy because he owned a horse which he used for transportation and ploughing. One day the horse ran away. All his neighbours said how terrible it was, but the farmer simply said, 'Maybe!' A few days later the horse returned and brought two wild horses with it. The neighbours were amazed at his good fortune, but the farmer just said 'Maybe.' The next day the farmer's son tried to ride one of the wild horses and fell off, breaking his leg. The neighbours offered their sympathy for his misfortune, but the farmer just said 'Maybe.' The next week conscription officers came to the village to take young men for the army. They rejected the farmer's son because of his broken leg. The neighbours said he was lucky, but once again, the farmer said 'Maybe.'

You are the one that gives meaning to every one of your experiences. When I was in my teens, my parents told me they were going away for the weekend and invited me to join them as well. I declined since I realised that that this could be a wonderful opportunity to have the house to myself for a whole weekend. I suspect that if you knew your parents were away for a few nights, like me, you would probably invite all your friends around for a party. And that's exactly what I did! We had a fantastic time, listening to music, watching movies, eating and drinking.

At around 2.00am, I noticed that quite a few of my friends had left and I was also feeling tired, so I said good-bye to the rest of my friends, turned off all the equipment downstairs, turned off the lights and went upstairs to bed. Just as I rolled over to fall asleep, I started to hear noises downstairs; noises that sounded like footsteps, and footsteps that led me to believe that there was an intruder in the house.

My first reaction was to dive under the covers, until I realised that I really was home alone and that if there was an intruder in the house, then I would have to be the one to deal with it. I pulled the covers down and

let my eyes adjust to the night light. By now, the footsteps were getting louder and closer. My heart was also beating louder and faster! In the corner of my room, I could make out the silhouette of my tennis racket so I crept quietly out of bed and reached for the racket and then made my way to the door. Taking a deep breath in, and with my tennis racket above my head, I threw open the door and ran down the landing.........
only to find that there was nobody there! And there never had been anybody there! My mind was playing tricks on me! It was actually the central heating pipes clicking and creaking, yet my mind had filtered and distorted that information so that I perceived it as footsteps and interpreted the footsteps as an intruder, giving myself a big adrenaline rush at the same time!

We sit in a room believing we are looking out of a window but actually we are looking into a mirror.

We respond to situations based on our filters – our own pair of tinted glasses - and according to our patterns from the past. By owning the mirror, we are in a position of responsibility to take back our power. We can literally choose to create our own reality!

> Just as we tend to assume that the world is as we see it, we naively suppose that people are as we imagine them to be. In this latter case, unfortunately, there is no scientific test that would prove the discrepancy between perception and reality. Although the possibility of gross deception is infinitely greater here than in our perception of the physical world, we still go on naively projecting our own psychology into our fellow human beings. In this way everyone creates for himself a series of more or less imaginary relationships based essentially on projection.
>
> 'General Aspects of Dream Psychology' (1916). In CW 8: The Structure and Dynamics of the Psyche. P.507
> **Carl Jung**

Imagine you are producing a theatrical show. Not only are you producing the show, you are also the director and the writer and this is a show of your life. Although there are actors and actresses involved in the production, you, of course, are the star and are in every single scene. It may not be in your conscious awareness, but you are also the writer, producer, director and the star of your life. At an unconscious level, you've brought in the other people in your life to take on various roles in your show. Away from the show, they too have their own lives to lead. But once they turn up at the theatre for your show, they leave that behind to become the character that you have assigned them in your show, and that they have agreed to play. Each and every person in your life is reflecting a part of yourself. Whatever they do or say in your show is a result of your script and how you choose to perceive them. You too are also in their show, and each of them projects something different onto you. Have you ever noticed that you act completely differently with various people? Or maybe you have a different persona at the workplace than you have at home with friends?

Just for a moment, think about your best friend. What qualities and characteristics do you admire? Those qualities are in you. Now bring to mind someone that you dislike. What qualities and characteristics do you dislike? Those qualities are also in you! What you are seeing outside is what you are projecting from the inside.

Think about this

In the film and documentary 'What The Bleep Do We Know', Candace Pert Ph.D (author of Molecules of Emotions) tells the tale of a native American Indian shaman, living on one of the Caribbean islands. Columbus' clipper ships were heading towards the island but because the shaman had no knowledge of the existence of clipper ships he couldn't see them. What he could see was that there were changes in the water and waves. Every day, he would look out to sea and notice the changes in the waves and water until finally he was able to see

Columbus' clipper ships. He went back inland and told his tribe about the existence of these ships and because they believed and trusted the Shaman, they too were able to see the clipper ships.

It was Mark Twain who said: 'It's never too late to have a happy childhood.' Do you look back and perceive your childhood as a struggle and focus on the not so good stuff or do you choose to remember the good times?

One of my friends was having his astrological chart read and was amazed at the accuracy at which the astrologer was describing his parents and siblings. How could he know so much about his parents when he was actually reading his chart? It didn't make sense, until the astrologer explained that he was describing my friend's parents and siblings on how he would choose to perceive them based on the information from his astrological chart!

In Gestalt Therapy, 'awareness is used to encourage personal growth and develop potential by noticing how we are living now and exploring how we may create any fixed patterns of behaviour that leave us feeling dissatisfied, uncomfortable or ill at ease.' Noticing what we experience and how we choose to behave in the present creates an opportunity to explore changes in our behaviour and attitudes now. This may enable us to complete previously unresolved experiences and to develop more satisfying ways of expressing ourselves and interacting with others. Differences in perspectives and how we choose to view and create our world become the focus of experimentation including understanding others' model of world. The goal is for us to become aware of what we are doing, how we are doing it and how we can change ourselves and at the same time, learn to accept and value ourselves.

When we add these new dimensions to our current perspective of the world, we learn new ways of behaving that enhance and enrich every relationship. On a personal level we can explore our relationships with partners and friends. In business, we can explore our relationship with managers, colleagues as well as customers and clients.

How can we do this? Dr. Stephen Covey says we should 'seek first to understand, then to be understood.' In other words, if we stand in someone else's shoes then we'll see what they see, hear what they hear, feel what they feel and understand the world from their perspective. This is the position of empathy and extremely useful in helping you step out of your current experience; gather information and check how your behaviour impacts other people and adjust it accordingly.

Imagine being able to think the way another person thinks and truly appreciate other people's feelings.

Jagat used this method to bring two friends back together. He told me that it started as a mild disagreement over a trivial matter. 'Then it became an argument before escalating into an all-out no-holds-barred name-calling war that stopped just short of physical violence. In that one moment the two girls, best friends for years, decided to cut themselves out of each other's lives.'

Jagat is a graduate from one of our NLP Master Practitioner programs and told me it was especially hard on him because they were his best friends too! 'I tried everything I could to get them to at least talk to each other, but nothing worked. That was when I decided to break my golden rule – 'never NLP your friends.' As it turned out, I'm glad I did.

'It was challenging, but I managed to persuade them both to meet me at a 'neutral venue'. They agreed whilst dramatically insisting that they would not 'be in the same room as that *****!'

'So while one sulked in the kitchen, I took the other through a process whereby she first experienced the situation through her own eyes and in her own model of the world. Next, I asked her to literally step out of her current experience and imagine the world through her former friend's eyes; to experience the argument and really see what she was seeing, hear what she was hearing, feel what she was feeling and notice what she was noticing. Next, I asked her to step back and imagine she was watching and listening to herself and her former friend arguing, like a fly on the wall, looking down on the situation and just noticing the behaviour the two of them were demonstrating, the beliefs they were both operating from and what was important to each of them. It was at that moment that she burst into tears at the stupidity of the argument! Then, leaving her to mop up her tears, I went through the same process with the other one in the kitchen.

'Forty-five minutes later, buckets of tears and a barrage of "I'm-so-sorry-it-was-all-my-fault's" later, the two were friends again. For one small moment, I was afraid they'd start another war over which one had behaved like the bigger idiot.'

'In the end, it all worked out just fine. We went out for dinner and a movie before hitting a local club where we stayed till they decided to throw us out . . . just like old times!'

Life does look a whole lot different when you step away from 'me, myself and I' and try seeing it through someone else's eyes for a change. Reshma said 'my greatest fear had always been that if I were to just be myself, people would see that and try to take advantage of it to hurt me. This made me put on one hellava show, and a lot of effort went into creating a person that I am not. Now it just doesn't matter anymore and I have a lot more faith in people as well. After all, they've got their own things going on and realising that has made me a lot less defensive and more open.'

I also used this same technique of stepping out of my current experience years ago when I was having trouble understanding a former colleague's action. I was training and delivering a public program and we'd just got to the part where I'd talked about the circle of control and influence; that there are certain things in life you can control and other areas where you have absolutely no control. At that very moment, officials from the Labour Department walked in and told me that I would have to go with them to the police department because I was working illegally. While I knew that my visa and papers were in order, at that moment there was no choice but to leave with the labour department officials until I could prove it. Basically, it felt like I was under arrest! I have no idea what the thirty or so delegates thought as I was marched off and while I remained calm and professional in the room, the anger and shock soon took over as we headed for the nearest police station. Of course, the whole matter was cleared up fairly quickly once they had seen my papers and visa, but I was furious that this should have happened at all. And I knew exactly who had caused the situation! We had previously worked together. Why would he do such a thing? And for what purpose would I have created this situation?

It was several years later that I was able to step into his shoes, and realised that in his model of the world I had violated what was important to him. I can laugh about it now but it's not an experience I would want to repeat. What's even more interesting is that despite the training coming to an abrupt halt, one of the delegates recommended and introduced me to her HR Manager. We subsequently met and secured them as a long-term client. Every cloud does have a silver lining!

For Debbie, stepping out of her current experience gave her insight into how her behaviour was impacting others. She was part of a semi-professional dance troupe when she was in her late teens and early twenties. She loved it and religiously attended every class and rehearsal to be the best that she could be and expected everyone in the group to be as conscientious as her and put in the time and effort. One summer the troupe was running through the final rehearsal for the evening show at a venue on the coast. At that time, the troupe had seen members leave and new members join over the years and tonight, Mariam was making her stage debut. Debbie and Mariam were on stage to start the first number and Debbie was quick to give Mariam feedback on her rehearsal performance. She was surprised when she went back to the changing rooms and found Mariam in tears and the rest of the group comforting her. Her surprise quickly turned to shame when she realised that she was the cause of Mariam's tears. She had no idea that she had upset Mariam with her direct and forthright feedback. Her intention had been to help Mariam and ensure that the show would be a great performance that evening. It was a big wake up call to check in and find out how her behaviour was affecting others. Since that time, Debbie has made a concerted effort to soften her approach and notice the response she gets from others.

In our programs, we often ask a delegate to sit, think of and re-live an emotionally charged situation (hopefully a positive situation), one that they can hold in their mind for at least five minutes. We then ask another delegate to adopt exactly the same physiology, gestures, breathing patterns, facial expressions until they are matching the first delegate exactly. After five minutes, they break this pattern and we ask the second delegate to 'guess' what the first delegate was thinking and feeling. It's amazing and uncanny at just how close and accurate they are in assessing the first delegates experience and emotions. When I first experienced this exercise, my partner was happily reliving a tense moment in a football match. While I correctly attuned to the fact that it was a football match, he was even more surprised when I said 'and did they just score a goal at the end?' They had and I had noticed a shift in his breathing and physiology to correctly assess that something had changed inside!

This ability to step out of your current experience and understand how your behaviour is affecting others and see what the other person is seeing, hear what the other person hears and feel what the other person is feeling is like having your own magic mirror.

Mahatma Gandhi is renowned as a master negotiator, and it's said that when he was in the UK to meet with the British government, he had another room set aside which he had laid out in the same seating as the main conference room. Every night he would sit in each of the seats to gain insight into the thinking of each of the delegates. This method of really getting into the shoes of all the other delegates and officials served him well in the negotiations and finally led to the freedom of India.

You can use the exact same technique to improve your relationships and improve rapport. But what if the situation is tense or you feel stuck or over-emotional? Now you need to hold that magic mirror from a distance - to step back, get some distance from the situation as if you're a fly on the wall.

Whenever I fly out of the country, I like to look out the window as the plane takes off. And as the plane soars higher, the houses become smaller, the cars shrink to matchbox size and people appear to be as small as ants. It's at that moment that I often put my cares and worries aside and say to myself, 'In the larger scale of things it doesn't really matter.' It helps me put any problems and anxieties back into their true perspective.

It's this detachment that can help you check the ecology of your goals and outcomes. (And by ecology, I mean that your goals and objectives should have a positive impact on you and those around you.)

Julie was working in Kuwait with her husband Hakim when they got caught in the Gulf Crisis, in August 1990. It was a terrifying time during the occupation, not knowing whether to stay put or attempt an escape. Julie and Hakim attempted the latter only to be held at gunpoint as they crossed the desert to Saudi Arabia. Having left all their worldly possessions behind they finally made it to Saudi Arabia where the British Embassy flew them back home. They later returned to the region to re-build their life together in the sports, health and fitness field and again enjoyed an expatriate lifestyle, looking forward to the arrival of children to complete their family unit. At only 41 years of age, Hakim unexpectedly collapsed with a heart aneurism after a game of squash and subsequently died. In that moment, Julie's whole life was dramatically and completely turned upside down. Everything they had been through together, everything they had planned together, their hopes and dreams of a family suddenly vanished. Although Julie threw herself back into work to keep going, she finally took a travel sabbatical in 1999: a time to reflect, refresh, re-focus and start the long climb over the wall of grief to the mountains and gardens of hope and new beginnings. At 5.30am on her 40th birthday she reached a peak. The peak was Mount Kinabalu; 4095 metres and the highest peak in South East Asia. It was there, on her first mountain summit, she looked down on the world from a completely new perspective and had an 'a-ha' moment as she fondly recalls it. She chose this moment as the beginning of a new life and the idea for her now very successful company, Mountain High! Not only did she climb the wall and peek over the top, Julie now helps hundreds of people climb to even greater heights, physically, mentally and emotionally.

'The greatest discovery in our generation is that human beings, by changing the inner attitudes of their minds, can change the outer aspects of their lives.'

So how can you step out of your current experience and use the magic mirror to gain insight into a problem or difficult situation involving others?

Changing the tint on your lens!

Think about a relationship that is important for you to improve or a challenging situation involving another person that you would like greater clarity on, and start remembering the situation and interaction.

1. Look at yourself in the mirror and see the situation and relationship through your own eyes, hearing your experience through your own ears and noticing how you feel about the situation and the other person. Ask yourself:

- What results am I getting from this relationship/situation?

- What's important to me about this relationship/situation?

- What beliefs am I operating from?

- Write down what are you learning about yourself and the other person

2. Turn the mirror so you see the experience through the other person's eyes and notice what you look like from this side of the mirror. Hear the experience through the other person's ears and listen to what you sound like and feel what it is like to be the other person and what you feel about yourself. As if you are the other person respond to the following questions:

- What results am I getting from the relationship/situation?

- What's important to me about the relationship/situation?

- What beliefs am I operating from?

- Write down what are you learning about yourself and the other person

3. Turn the mirror towards yourself and the other person and experience the situation/relationship as a detached observer, like a 'fly on the wall' so that you can see yourself and the other person, hear the two of them talking and notice their behaviour and interaction. Go through the following questions:

- What results are we getting from the relationship/situation?

- What's important to us about the relationship/situation?

- What beliefs are we operating from?

- Write down what are you learning about yourself and the other person

4. Imagine the next time you will be in this situation or in this relationship and notice how the situation/relationship has changed and what you will do differently next time.

Aidan, a senior manager, was attending one of our short introductory programs and early during the program had complained of stress in his work life. In the afternoon we run through the above exercise;

first stepping out of your current experience and gathering different information on a difficult situation involving another person, viewing the situation from your own viewpoint, secondly, by stepping into the other person's shoes. The latter often feels like arguing against yourself. And finally, stepping away from the situation to see and hear the situation detached from the emotions. Nine months earlier, Aidan and another senior manager within his organisation had had a serious disagreement. So serious that neither of them had spoken to each other since, which was causing them both a great deal of stress and having a negative effect on their work and respective departments. Aidan went through the situation from his own viewpoint and then stood in the shoes of this other senior manager. However, when he completely stepped back from the situation – fly on the wall position - he looked at himself and the other manager and simply said, 'what a pair of idiots.' At that moment, he told me, all the stress he'd been dealing with for the last nine months instantly vanished! He also made a commitment to speak with the other manager the next day and says that the exercise transformed the way he now works!

Everyone has something different to teach us. Everyone has a different perspective; an additional viewpoint, another angle. You never know who might be the next source of inspiration for you!

What you're now learning is to take a different position, to reflect the mirror at a different angle on a situation or a relationship in order to find a balance in climbing over the wall to a solution.

The little creature just let go! He let go and the current swept him away! At first he was scraped along the bottom of the river bed, and then he was knocked into other rocks. There were moments where he wondered if he had made the right choice, but all of a sudden, the current lifted him up and he felt he was flying through the water as joy and excitement surged in his heart. After awhile, the current slowed down and all became calm and when he opened his eyes, everything looked fresh and completely new!

Remember, it's our patterns in thinking and behaviour and our filters that we project onto the world that create our response to circumstances, not the circumstances themselves.

Chapter 6

A GARDEN OF OPPORTUNITY

A GARDEN OF OPPORTUNITY

The time had come to prepare the soil and sow the seeds for next year's harvest. Two seeds lay just beneath the soil where the gardener had placed them and waited as the autumn days passed. The gardener occasionally turned the soil as birds pecked at the earth searching for worms. As autumn turned to winter the two seeds huddled together to keep warm. The winter nights grew longer, the days became colder and even below the surface, the two seeds knew that changes were taking place above them. At times the ground was damp and wet from the rain and they sank deeper down into the earth. And sometimes the ground was rock hard from the north winds and bitter frost. At one point they felt the weight of the winter snow piled above them, and still they huddled closer together and waited.

Time passed, the snow began to melt and water seeped below the surface to reach the two seeds. They began to move again as winter turned to spring and a warm breeze brushed over the soil. The seeds began to feel a sense of excitement, a sense of anticipation that something more was about to happen. 'I wonder what's up there?' thought the first little seed, as she began to push little green shoots up, curious to reach the light. 'And I wonder what's even deeper down,' she whispered as she began to push tiny roots further down into the soil.

The second seed said, 'We don't know what's up there. It could be dangerous and scary. Maybe we should stay here a little longer. Yes, I think I'll stay here a little longer.'

> The stiffest tree is most easily cracked while the willow survives by bending beneath the wind.

It's easy to stay where you are, isn't it? And there are plenty of excuses too, such as do you have all the resources you require to be successful? Or do you have the information you need? Do you have what it takes?

The fact is, you will never have all the information you require, so in the words of Richard Branson, 'screw it, and let's do it!' The universe is made up of uncertainty so if you wait until you have all that you require in order to be 100% sure, you'll never do anything! So why not do it anyway? And while we're talking about Richard Branson, you might want to remember that he started off selling mail order records through a student magazine and using a telephone box as his office!

The most successful people in the world did not wake up one morning to find success sitting at their doorstep waiting to come in. They had to go out into the world, keep going and make it happen!

Oprah Winfrey stands as a role model for millions, not only in the world of media and entertainment but also in the larger realm. An estimated 14 million viewers daily in the US and millions more in 132 countries around the globe tune in to her talk show and her personal fortune is estimated at more than half a billion dollars. She owns her own production company which creates feature films, prime-time TV specials and home videos. On top of that, she won an Academy Award nomination for her role in 'The Colour Purple'. Turn the clock back and you would have found a lonely child raised by her grandmother on a poor farm who found solace in books. It was her interest in books that won her a scholarship to a better school and her talent for public performance that gave her the first taste of public attention. From radio she went on to become the first black TV-news anchor and in 1984 moved on to host A.M. Chicago which went on to become The Oprah Winfrey Show. Not only is she an icon of success, Oprah encourages viewers to improve their lives and the world at large; she makes people care because she cares.

One of my friends told me that Oprah is one of her role models because 'she speaks and lives her truth. She has courage, compassion and is "real" while reaching out to others.'

The point is that while Richard Branson and Oprah Winfrey are household names and icons of success, just like you and me, they have also hit brick walls and barriers – and still do! What they do that you may not be doing yet, is to look at the brick walls and barriers as opportunities and to learn to notice the results of what they do, have a willingness to change their behaviour....... and keep going! In other words, there's no such thing as failure, only feedback........and learning!

One of my own role models of excellence, Robert Smith, was in my part of the world recently. A master trainer of NLP and a master communicator, we organised a short, but well-attended seminar. As we headed to dinner to celebrate its success, I was surprised when he asked me for feedback. Here was one of my role models asking for feedback from little ol' me! Robert told me he always reviews and gives himself feedback and it's now something that has become a habit for me after every seminar and training. 'What did I do well? What could I do differently to make it even better?'

Just for a moment, ask yourself:

- What are you doing well?

- What could you do differently to be even better?

Feedback truly is the breakfast of champions and as Robert is fond of saying, 'do what you do best, and do it well!'

"Every wrong attempt discarded is another step forward!"
Edison

Remember, it's your wall, your journey and your choice of the way through! So right now, think about all the times in your life when you have been successful; maybe you received a promotion, passed an exam at school or college, learnt something really quickly and easily or came up with a great new idea. Why is it important to keep track of all the times you've been successful in the past? Because you can re-create that same success right now! It really is a garden of opportunity!

You have a strategy for literally everything that you do including:-

Creativity	Getting up in the morning	Relaxation
Wealth		Stress
	Success	
Learning		Love
	Motivation	
Attraction		Depression
	Deciding	
Happiness		Confidence
	Health	

..........and everything else!

How many of you have used a strategy today? Actually, you're using your strategies all the time but most people are not aware of their use of strategies. But we are creatures of patterns and habits. Remember how quickly we get stuck in our comfort zone of doing the same things every single day and in the same way? Our entire lives follow patterns that we take with us wherever we go and it's these patterns that create our responses to situations. Are all of your patterns useful and serving to help you get the results you want or is it time to re-evaluate and let go of the less than useful ones?

Two monks were on a sacred pilgrimage. They were from a particular order that clearly forbade that they speak to or touch women so the two of them had chosen a route avoiding busy towns and villages. They had walked for many miles in the rainy season and were hoping that the river ahead of them would not be impassable. But the river had burst its banks and neither the boatman nor the boat were anywhere to be found. A woman dressed in fine clothes and holding an umbrella stood by the river and urged the two monks to help her cross the river as she urgently needed to reach the other side.

The younger monk chose to ignore her and looked away, maintaining adherence to his vows. The elder monk also said nothing but swept her up onto his shoulders and carried her across the river and safely put her down on the other side.

Hours later, the younger monk was still telling the older monk off and accusing him of betraying his order and betraying his vows. How dare he? How could he? What a thing to do!

Eventually, the two monks entered a clear field and the elder monk stopped and turned to look at the younger monk. After a long moment of silence, he quietly said: 'I put that woman down hours ago and you, my brother, are still carrying her!'

Are you running and re-running the same patterns of behaviour that no longer serve you? There are effective strategies and ineffective strategies. By becoming aware of your effective strategies you can begin to achieve your goals, choose the life you want and access the triggers to success anytime, anyplace, and anywhere.

If you want to drive your car effectively you need to first check that the gear is in neutral and then turn the key in the ignition. If you want flowers to grow in your garden, you need to prepare the ground first and then plant the seeds. If you want to call a friend, you need to dial the telephone number in exactly the right sequence. If you want to produce a gourmet meal, you need to buy the ingredients first and follow each step of the recipe in the correct sequence. If you've been successful in the past what had to happen first? What was the very first thing that had to happen? Following the same pattern in the same sequence will always give you the same result. Are you consistently producing the results you want in your life?

The dictionary defines a strategy as 'a carefully devised plan of action to achieve a goal, or the art of developing or carrying out such a plan.' Or think about it as the key to success; to simply unlock the door and walk through that wall! Once you understand your strategy you'll know how you created success in the past and can re-create it again and again!

A strategy is really a specific way to organise your resources whether those resources are money, relationships, attraction, health & fitness, love, relaxation or time. Are there specific ways to organise your money that will give you more money or less money? Are there specific ways to attract others and specific ways to turn them off? Are there specific ways to stay fit and healthy? Are there specific ways to feel calm and relaxed? You bet! Are there specific ways to get your relationship back on track?

Meg had been married for 20 years and had suspected for two years that her marriage was in trouble. Friends had given her hints that her husband was seeing someone overseas and while she initially tried to ignore these hints, she decided to pursue the truth in order to confront him. 'I let it go on too long and should have trusted my instincts, but I didn't. A part of me didn't want to rock the boat while another part of me knew that something was wrong. Once I had enough evidence and my husband couldn't refuse or deny it, then I decided that I could start to deal with the truth. My initial strategy was to stay in the house and sort things out, but the truth was that my home had been violated. This woman had been in my house and I had a feeling that I needed to leave. I also felt that my marriage was worth saving and as it turned out; my husband also felt the same. We made an agreement that if he would make me financially viable so that I could stay in the country, we would go to counselling.'

'The next step in my strategy was to find a neutral place that didn't have a feel of home about it so that I didn't become attached to it. I then created a very quiet, 'zen' place and didn't even tell my husband where it was. I made a decision to have time to myself and to look after my needs only. This included further studies as a yoga teacher and to train to be a yoga therapist as well as writing another book. I'd put off this course for a long time by putting other people's needs before my own and now, because of the infidelity, I put my needs first. It was the right thing to do. After 16 years of teaching yoga I'd reached a rut and I needed to grow and to develop new methods of teaching. I also needed to process a lot of the anger, resentment and jealousy and the program I attended was all about processing your emotions on the yoga mat. My life was mirroring what I was studying! I was reaching out to make sense of what was happening to me. I also decided to be celibate for 3 months while we went through counselling because sex can be a very easy tool to use when you're in a divorce or separation situation. I wanted to stand back emotionally and be detached at that time and look at my marriage and understand where it was going.'

'So I had my space and a core group of friends, who knew I was staying in my marriage. My husband and I had a lot of history together of solving problems and we believed we could use those strategies and experience to get through this. However, after six months on my own we were still not able to validate each other's value to the marriage and I needed to be validated as a person and contributor to the marriage. I was a great wife, great mother, great friend, great socialiser and a part of me is also a yoga teacher. That was something that he had never acknowledged or appreciated. I encouraged him to make some space for the person I was and to acknowledge that it was a big part of my life. My philosophy is that if you cannot be yourself in a relationship, it's costing you too much. Move on and move out.'

'An important part of my strategy was that regardless of what happened in the future of our marriage, I wanted to be financially secure. That was important to me. The final factor in moving back in was that I needed to see that he was sorry and that he understood the hurt he had caused and was willing to make amends for that. I also needed to be able to have gone through enough self-healing to feel that I forgave him as there would have been no point going back into the relationship always looking over my shoulder. I needed to be 100% present in the relationship in order for it to work and move forward. I worked all that out and there was a moment when I felt I didn't need to forgive him, but needed to forgive myself for not picking up on things before. Once I realised that it was about forgiving myself, then I could move back in.'

'We now have a very definite strategy that when we're apart, we're apart. But when we're together we commit to being around together. We've also learnt to explore the idea that when we do disagree about things we do not back each other into a corner and give ultimatums. The relationship has improved a lot; it has changed the way we relate and has made it richer. As for myself, I no longer have a fear of abandonment which frees me up to enjoy the relationship a lot more.'

One of the most important parts of Meg's strategy was to do with the fact she lives in an expatriate environment where anything goes. 'I'd seen so many people put up with bad behavior just for the sake of keeping the family together, or for financial security.' Meg decided it was important to make a stand and not to compromise. The behaviour was not acceptable.

Are there specific ways to create health and fitness? Deana thinks so! Her story begins shortly after she started a new dream job with a small company. 'The company was still short of cash and I had put together some ideas for marketing within a small budget and as a result, was given the position for marketing in addition to my other responsibilities. I had also introduced a good friend to my employer who might be able to help with writing some articles for the local press. Unbeknown to me my so-called "good friend" and another friend got together and presented a strategy to my employer with a view to pitching for my new position. I had no idea that my "friends" had gone behind my back, while my employer assumed that I was not keen on staying with the company and was suggesting someone else to do the job. I cannot begin to explain how I felt when I found out what had been going on. I ran the full gamut of emotions. Shock initially, followed by anger and betrayal by two close friends. How could they do such a thing? Didn't they know how hurt and upset I would be? Didn't they value our friendship? Obviously not! I also remember the physical sensations that accompanied these emotions as gut wrenching and stomach churning. Amongst these was also the feeling that the wonderful experience of my new job had turned sour in an instant.'

'With such a close social network my strategy was to avoid the places and situations where we would possibly meet to minimise further distress. This worked for awhile, but then I fell ill. I was diagnosed with a variety of conditions until I finally went to see a gynaecologist and was diagnosed with an abscess in my lower abdomen. One of the first questions my doctor asked was if I had recently had a shock as this can often have a profound effect on the immune system. Until this point, I hadn't seen the connection between the two events but it did seem that I had manifested something. Surgery was considered the only solution - quickly too - and the paperwork was sent to the hospital.'

'I was not happy to have surgery which could mean the removal of the ovary in question so whilst I waited for my appointment I decided to take responsibility and investigate alternative routes to deal with the problem. I looked at what was already working and adapted my regular yoga practice using techniques for the pain and relaxation and worked on my diet in response to allergy testing. In addition, I decided to adopt a positive approach to the whole process. Out of curiosity and the recommendation of a friend I attended a series of personal development sessions that literally lifted me out of the situation and allowed me to observe what had happened from a distance without being sucked into the emotions and events that seemed to cloud my vision. I could see that I was not a victim of events and that I could change the way I viewed and experienced the event to create a new outcome. In addition, I could harness my thoughts to bring about an emotional and mental transformation that would begin the healing process.'

'I used these new techniques I was given and combined them with my own strategy for relaxing and creating a nurturing yoga practice, continuing to work on myself with renewed enthusiasm.'

'A few weeks later, when I returned to the doctor for a check-up it was discovered that my hospital paperwork had been mislaid and I had missed the window of opportunity with a visiting surgeon. I also found out, to the doctors delight and amazement, that the cyst and abscess were now so reduced that surgery was not required.'

Deana also told me that not long after her recovery, both 'friends' moved away!

Josh told me that his brother is one of his role models in business. 'He's a multi-millionaire and his business strategy is one I follow myself. Simply to 'make yourself redundant.' To do that he has to make the people and systems so efficient that he is no longer needed in that role. That left him free to:

1) Take off the whole school summer holidays to be with his family, plus skiing holidays in the winter.

2) Become a champion sailor: he has won the European Micro-Multihull Championship and both the Around the Island (Isle of Wight) Race and the Around Great Britain Race

3) Develop his business in different ways to become the dominant force in the industry by a huge margin

4) Get involved in lobbying at the European Parliament to influence legislation that could affect his industry

5) Build a huge 6-bedroom house in Cornwall with a cellar that acts as both a games room and party room and big enough to have a 25-metre shooting range in it, plus a 5-bedroom house with the biggest garden just south of London.

And did I mention that he left school at 15 to become an apprentice electrician earning about 3 pounds a week!

'In my own business,' Josh went on, 'my belief is that people intrinsically want to work, to learn and to achieve, and that most so-called management strategies actually de-motivate, confuse and hamper them. So my strategy is to manage by not-managing. I just explain our business model and what we need to achieve in order to be successful and then we try and figure it out as we go along. When people visit the office when I am out or on vacation, they later tell me everyone works exactly the same whether I am there or not.'

Understanding *YOUR* strategies for success means that you will be able to recreate anything great you've ever done. If you've ever been creative, happy, healthy or motivated and confident, wouldn't it be useful to be able to find the right button to press for success? And anything you've done more than once you can do it again.

Our local newspaper recently ran a feature on a couple of successful local entrepreneurs. Despite the challenges of setting up a business overseas they all cited that flexibility was key to their success strategy, and an absolute passion for what they do. An important strategy also included never taking 'no' for an answer, discovering new ways to resolve issues while keeping focused on the business objectives. All those interviewed said that you have to believe in yourself and be self-motivated!

So what gets you up in the morning? What gets you excited about the day ahead? What would be some useful hot buttons to get you going as you tunnel, break through or climb over that wall? How about discovering your motivation strategy to give you a kick start?

Finding the hot buttons to give you a kick start!

1. Imagine you are about to go on a journey; an important journey of discovery and you want to be motivated right now. Think about the best holiday you ever went on, that you really enjoyed and that you knew was the right one for you. Or maybe you can think back to another time in the past when you were totally motivated. As you go back to that time now, what was the very first thing that caused you to be totally motivated?

- Was it something you saw (or the way someone looked at you?)

- Was it something you heard (or someone's tone of voice?)

- Was it the touch of someone or something?

What was the very first thing that caused you to be totally motivated? And after you (saw, heard or felt) that, what was the very next thing that happened as you were totally motivated?

- Did you picture something in your mind?

- Say something to yourself, or hear something?

- Have a certain feeling or emotion?

Notice what you see, hear and feel and become curious about the order and sequence. Have you ever watched a top athlete preparing for an event? They go through exactly the same motivation sequence to get themselves revved up! You can rev yourself up to the best possible mental and emotional state once you understand your own motivation sequence!

Making the right choice!

2. a. How did you decide that was the holiday for you? How did you choose from all the different options between a beach holiday, sightseeing, cultural tour or adventure trekking in the Himalayas? As you go back to a time in the past when you made a decision that you were pleased with and that you now know was a good decision, ask yourself how you decided that was the specific (holiday, car, house) for you? Notice what you see, hear and feel.

b. Think about something you have to make a choice about. This could be about finding a different job, buying an expensive item or to do with a relationship. Ask yourself, 'What's important to me in choosing this new job (or expensive item etc)?' and write down the answers. In deciding between your choices, notice what you see, hear and feel for each of the choices right now, in 6 months' time, in one year's time and notice the finer distinctions.

c. Compare a and b and notice which of your choices most closely matches the strategy of a and this is the one for you!

By becoming aware of our use of these keys and triggers to success that we have used in the past to make good choices, we can begin to choose the life we want.

What you've done by tunnelling, breaking through and climbing over the wall is to find out what's important to you and what drives you. You now know that what we believe about ourselves forms our thoughts, and our thoughts create feelings that lead to behaviours which become habits. You've challenged your dream stoppers and have hopefully replaced them with some powerful new ones that do serve you in achieving what you want. And since all the world is a stage, you can now create the actors and actresses on that stage and the relationships you have with each and every one of them.

How do you know if you've got it all right? Simple! Test it! And that's exactly what Thomas Edison did when he invented the first light bulb. It was also reported that he found one thousand, nine hundred and ninety-nine ways how not to make a light bulb! How do you know when the cake is cooked? Test it and taste it! New walls come up and within them lay our greatest opportunities for growth. My mother shared with me, 'When I am at a low ebb and feel at a wall, it is always because I have not found another dream to accomplish and that means I sometimes stay at the wall for longer than I should.' So keep moving!

I've always thought it would be great if a client came to see me to assist them in, for example, reaching their ideal weight and I was able to say that I could lose it for them. 'Give it to me,' I could say, 'I'll lose it for you so that you will never be able to find it!' Many people believe that by attending personal empowerment programs or by reading a self development book that their life is suddenly going to change into some sort of nirvana and nothing bad will ever happen to them again in life. What it really means is that you have more choice and more flexibility to deal with the walls and challenges that do occur.

Can I lose the weight for you, find you a new job, ensure you're in a better relationship? No, but what I can do is find out what will motivate you to achieve your ideal weight, find a new job or ensure your next relationship is better by eliciting your values and ensuring they are aligned with your goals, assisting you to uncover the dream stoppers that are holding you back and gaining a deeper awareness of who you really are and who you want to be. The responsibility for the results you get lies entirely with you. That means that if you're successful it's your fault!

The journey of a thousand miles really does begin with the first step. So imagine that you took the first step and kept going. So look around you right now. What does your garden look like? Is it filled with flowers in full bloom or is it an orchard in the first throes of spring? Maybe it grows aromatic herbs and nutritious vegetables, or maybe it's a playground with adventure swings and slides.

'Wow! What a difference 3 days can make!' Rania just said to me over our lengthy telephone conversation. Last week when I spoke with her all was doom and gloom. Should she leave the country and go back to the UK, and if she did where would she live and what would she do? After 15 years with an international airline, she has found it difficult to adjust to 'life on the ground' and carve herself a new career. Friendly, energetic and recently divorced, she moved into commission-only property sales just as the market went into a lull and has struggled to make ends meet. Her landlord has moved back into the villa she rented and it has proved a challenging combination with the landlord's dogs fighting with tenants' cats amongst other things. Pipes bursting and sinks blocked have not helped alleviate already high stress levels and three days ago she desperately needed to find alternative accommodation. The choice was between two expensive villas! And here we are, three days later as she prepares to move into a spacious reasonably priced property and a commission cheque awaiting collection! A reminder to us all that those brick walls can appear ....and disappear!

What you've discovered within that brick wall are opportunities and your own keys to success. Once you understand your specific keys and triggers to success you can start to recreate anything great you've ever done. And that means you may have to think of things differently from how you used to think of things before you opened this book.

So just take a few moments right now to notice all the things you're learning about yourself and how you'll start to use these tools and techniques to get the results you want. How you can break through that brick wall to get what you want simply by changing who you are and to change who you are by simply changing the way you choose to think and act. And as you do, notice all the new opportunities and gifts that are starting to present themselves, not now necessarily, but at least by the time you've turned the last page of this book, and how they can have lasting, profound and beneficial effects which can stay with you for the rest of life.

The first seed had already gone ahead and pushed her way through the soil to inhale her first breath of spring air and warm sunshine. There were other flowers, plants, shrubs and the sweet smells of fruit in blossom and aromas of a nearby herb garden. She pushed her roots deep to draw energy, nourishment and strength from the richness of the environment.

The second seed remained below, worrying that it could be dangerous above and below. 'I'll just stay here a little longer.' And continued with its risk-free strategy.

By the end of spring, the first little seed grew strong and tall, flourishing with a new sense of achievement and accomplishment. Her roots were strong and centred giving her a firm foundation on which to become even stronger and greater.

Only you can make the choices and the changes and now you've created new ways to get the results you want!

What treasures lie inside of you?

'When we recognize our nature, we become free from suffering. Whether you recognize it or not, though, its qualities remain unchanged. But when you begin to recognize it in yourself, you change, and the quality of your life changes as well. Things you never dreamed possible begin to happen.'
Yongey Mingyur Rinpoche
(often referred to as 'the happiest man on earth.')

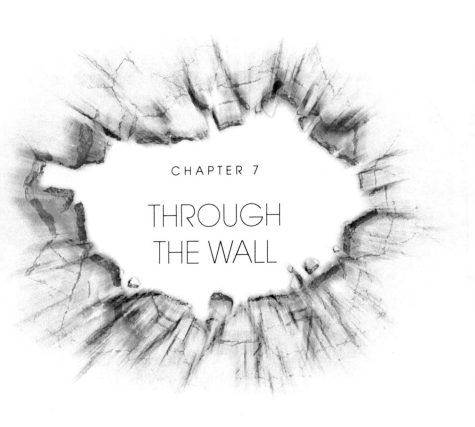

CHAPTER 7

THROUGH
THE WALL

THROUGH THE WALL!

Have you ever had an amazing and incredible dream? Have you ever tried to explain that dream to a friend and they just didn't understand what you meant? Have you ever found a joke so funny, yet when you told it to others they just didn't get it? Or maybe you went on an amazing journey but just couldn't find the words to explain its impact on you? No matter how green and ripe the apple, you need to bite into it to really know how juicy and sweet it really is. In other words, it's better to paint the picture rather than run the gallery and when the planning is complete to be an artist of living! While we have over 615,000 words at our disposal and I was tempted to write more, what you now have is a set of actions, tools and techniques to play with, points to ponder and decisions to make in order to get you started in making your own journey through your wall. And as you continue your journey I hope you'll consider joining us at one of our experiential programs very soon.

Dream your dreams as they are the magic in our minds that cause wonderful things to happen!

Wishing you a wonderful journey!

ABOUT THE AUTHOR

Carol Talbot is an enthusiastic, energetic and versatile consultant. She has a strong personal interest in holistic development, accelerated learning and the health and fitness arena, and is a Neuro-linguistic programming (NLP) Certified Trainer, Trainer of Hypnosis & Time Line Therapy® and Master Firewalk Instructor. She lives in Dubai and loves the multi-cultural environment as well as 365 days of sunshine! A student of learning, she travels frequently and has shared these tools and techniques in Europe, Africa, India and the Middle East assisting others to break through their own walls. Her seminars and workshops are informal, creating a fun and relaxed environment, yet sharply focused, developing delegates' long-term strategies for personal development and growth.

EXPERIENTIAL PROGRAMS:

- Achieving Personal Excellence

- Transforming Teams

- Leadership Development

- NLP Programs for Personal & Professional Development

- Recharge your Life!

- Fire walking seminars & workshops

www.matrix-training.com

REFERENCES:

The Magic of Metaphor – Nick Owens

Molecules of Emotion – Candace Pert Ph.D

The People Puzzle – Morris Massey

Mission Possible – Kenneth Blanchard

The Secrets of a Millionaire Mind – T. Harv Eker

The 7 Habits of Highly Effective People – Dr Stephen R. Covey

The 8th Habit – Dr Stephen R. Covey

Flow: The Psychology of Optimal Experience – Mihaly Csikszentmhalyi

Illusions – Richard Bach

The Holographic Universe – Michael Talbot

The Field – Lynne McTaggart

NLP at Work – Sue Knight

Time Line Therapy & the Basis of Personality – Tad James & Wyatt Woodsmall

The NLP Workbook – Joseph O'Connor

Awaken the Giant Within – Anthony Robbins

Unlimited Power – Anthony Robbins

Screw It! Let's Do It! – Richard Branson

Lightning Source UK Ltd.
Milton Keynes UK
23 September 2010

160257UK00001B/76/P